THE BEAR

Look for these and other books in the
Lucent Endangered Animals and Habitats Series:

The Amazon Rain Forest
The Bald Eagle
The Bear
The Elephant
The Giant Panda
The Gorilla
The Manatee
The Oceans
The Rhinoceros
Seals and Sea Lions
The Shark
The Tiger
The Whale
The Wolf

Other related titles in the Lucent Overview Series:

Acid Rain
Endangered Species
Energy Alternatives
Garbage
The Greenhouse Effect
Hazardous Waste
Ocean Pollution
Oil Spills
Ozone
Pesticides
Population
Rainforests
Recycling
Saving the American Wilderness
Vanishing Wetlands
Zoos

THE BEAR

BY LAURA BARGHUSEN

Endangered
Animals &
Habitats

LUCENT BOOKS, INC.
SAN DIEGO, CALIFORNIA

LUCENT *Overview Series*

Library of Congress Cataloging-in-Publication Data

Barghusen, Laura, 1964–
    The bear / by Laura Barghusen.
        p.   cm. — (Endangered animals & habitats) (Lucent
overview series)
    Includes bibliographical references (p.   ) and index.
    Summary: Discusses the bears of the world and threats to their
existence, such as hunting and international trade, habitat
destruction, and captivity, as well as the future of bears.
    ISBN 1-56006-394-7 (lib. bdg. : alk. paper)
    1. Bears—Juvenile literature.   2. Endangered species—Juvenile
literature.   [1. Bears.   2. Endangered species.]   I. Title.   II. Series.
III. Series: Lucent overview series.
QL737.C27B357   1999
599.78—dc21   98-50214
                                                                          CIP
                                                                          AC

Contents

Introduction

BEARS HAVE EXCITED the imaginations of people for centuries, and many authors have noted that bears remind people of themselves. Like humans, bears walk by pressing their heels into the ground, and if something catches their attention, they may stand upright for a better look. Bears seek out nuts, berries, fruits, meat, fish, and other foods also prized by people. Sometimes they are playful, behaving very much like human children. Biologist Stephen Herrero writes about observing a grizzly bear playing:

> An older male was once seen crossing a snowslope in spring. He paused briefly to look down the slope, and then launched himself onto it, rolling and sliding down. At the bottom he shook himself, looked back up the slope, the top of which was hundreds of meters above him, and then climbed up and slid down again.[1]

In spite of these similarities, or perhaps because of them, people and bears have come into conflict in the modern world as they compete for space and for the same limited resources. Some bears are massive creatures and make formidable adversaries, frightening and challenging people with their sheer size and strength. Many species threaten human food supplies as well, devouring crops or attacking livestock.

A question of attitude

Humans respond to bears with a variety of attitudes. Bears are seen as powerful symbols of vanishing wild areas by those who value them as part of the wilderness as a whole, while other people regard bears as dangerous obstacles to their personal safety or economic well-being. In many areas, bears have been hunted to near extinction by those who consider them adversaries to be killed and proudly displayed as trophies.

Traditional Native American cultures used the organs of bears in rituals, which were often aimed at ensuring that bears would remain available to be hunted for skins and food. People in Asian cultures have traditionally used bear

A grizzly bear and cub stand on their hind legs to get a better view of their surroundings. Bears spend a lot of time—as humans do— on two feet.

organs and secretions for medicinal purposes, creating a continuous market for the skills of the bear hunter. Although for centuries bear losses occurred at a sustainable rate, with enough bears surviving to maintain healthy numbers, today the demands of a quickly growing human population are depleting bear populations dramatically. People are also moving into more and more of the areas where bears live and changing the habitat so that it is no longer as suitable for the animals' survival. The polar bear, which spends much of its life on the Arctic sea ice and the shores of Arctic waters, is the only bear whose original habitat appears to be beyond the reach of human intrusion. But even that may change as people consider exploring for fossil fuels along the coastlines where bears make their winter dens, and as human pollutants make their way into the bears' remote environments.

An adult polar bear stands with his back to his dinner, a freshly killed seal. The polar bear is one of the few bears whose natural habitat remains little altered by humans.

A question of ignorance, a question of time

Despite evidence from primitive art that people have been aware of bears for thousands of years, relatively little is known about these fascinating mammals and their habits. This is especially true of bears living outside North America like the sloth bears, Asiatic black bears, sun bears, and spectacled bears. This lack of knowledge means that the public often understands little or nothing about their plight as bear populations shrink and become isolated on smaller and smaller patches of remaining habitat. Even people genuinely interested in the conservation of bears often have trouble designing plans to help them because so little is known about their needs.

For bears in many areas, conservation is just getting started. Yet from the point of view of survival for many bears, it is already late in the game. Moreover, bears are not the only creatures that are becoming scarce in today's world. The populations of many other species are declining as people expand over the land and change the animals' habitats. There is evidence that nations are becoming increasingly concerned about the rapid loss of natural areas and native species, and want to make changes to preserve their natural resources. It is possible that these changes will also benefit bears.

1

Bears of the World

BEARS HAVE ROAMED the earth for more than 20 million years. The earliest were carnivores and bears are still classified as carnivores today, although most now eat a diet that is largely vegetarian. The first bears were only about the size of a fox, but today's bears tend to be large with powerful limbs, short tails, and round erect ears. The polar bears and the biggest brown bears are considered the largest land-dwelling carnivores living today.

The bears of today's world form a diverse group, with different species occupying a variety of habitats. These habitats range from the icy Arctic, which is home to the polar bear, to the tropical rain forests found along the equator, which are home to the sun bear. Different species of bear also have very different ways of life. For example, polar bears survive by hunting seals on the frozen seas, while sun bears climb forest trees to find fruits, honey, and small animals to eat.

In spite of this diversity in habitat and ways of life, all species of bear face some common problems that jeopardize their continued survival in the modern world. These problems, which have reduced the number of bears in many populations, include the destruction and alteration of familiar habitats, and the efficient hunting that became possible with modern firearms. Habitat destruction and hunting have especially serious consequences for bears because they need a lot of space and because they reproduce slowly.

Bears need large amounts of food, and in many cases vast territories in which to forage if they are to survive. All bear species except the polar bear are primarily vegetarian,

eating mainly berries, roots, nuts, and fruits. To get all the energy they need from such a diet, bears must locate and consume a lot of these small items. Although their vision has been described by some biologists as poor, and by others as similar in quality to our own, bears have an excellent sense of smell, which they often employ to locate food.

Bears are agile creatures with strong swimming abilities. Some species enter the water to forage for fish, and polar bears may actually stalk seals in the water or dive for kelp. Bears are also agile and quick on land. Grizzly bears can run as fast as thirty miles per hour to capture prey such as moose, elk, and other hooved mammals. The smaller bear species are adept at tree climbing and often forage for the nuts, fruits, or buds they find there. All bears have five toes on each paw, with a powerful claw extending from each toe. These claws aid them in subduing prey, digging for such items as ants and roots, and climbing trees.

Bears show considerable patience and ingenuity while foraging. In *Bears,* Helen Gilks describes the behavior of a hunting polar bear: "To catch a seal on the ice, a polar bear gradually creeps toward it. The bear keeps its body close to the ground, stopping if the seal opens its eyes, until the bear is near enough to charge."[2] Bear cubs learn complex feeding strategies from their mothers during their first few years of life. Once they are old enough to be on their own, they continue to develop new feeding strategies through their curiosity, intelligence, and ability to learn from experience. They may then pass these new strategies on to their own cubs. In *Bears: Majestic Creatures of the Wild,* Andrew E. Derocher and Ian Stirling describe how some brown bears in Alaska and Canada have learned to prey on caribou:

> Although bears cannot outrun caribou over long distances, they can ambush animals at places such as river crossings. Large canine teeth and powerful jaws enable a bear to kill a caribou quickly once it makes contact. Hunting caribou in this fashion was probably only practiced by a small number of bears at first and then learned by cubs watching their mothers.[3]

Smaller bears, such as this black bear, climb trees to forage for food.

The need for large areas in which to forage brings bears into direct competition with people as the human population grows, occupies more land area, and harvests more of the natural resources upon which bears depend, such as forest trees. Difficulty in securing adequate amounts of food due to shrinking habitats may result in the animals' starving or not eating enough to create the fat deposits essential for successful hibernation and reproduction. It may also lead to bears' learning to feed on human crops and livestock, increasing conflict between people and bears.

Bears as threatened species

There are seven species of bear existing today. This number does not include the giant panda, whose classification is disputed. Bears belong to the family Ursidae (pronounced Ur-sid-day), from the Latin word *ursus,* meaning "bear"; the adjective "ursine" is often used to describe bearlike traits. Each species has both a scientific name and one or more common names, such as "polar bear." The scientific name consists of the names of the genus and the species to which that bear belongs. For example, the polar bear belongs to the genus *Ursus* and the species *maritimus,* and thus its scientific name is *Ursus maritimus.* Some bears with the same scientific name are called by different common names in different regions. For example, brown bears, grizzly bears, and Kodiak bears all belong to the same species, *arctos,* but "grizzly bear" is the common name for *Ursus arctos* living in the United States and Canada, except those in the coastal areas stretching from British Columbia to the Alaska Peninsula, which are called "brown bears." "Brown bear" is also the common name for *Ursus arctos* living in Europe, Asia, and the Middle East. Finally, *Ursus arctos* on the Kodiak, Afognak, and Shuyak Islands of Alaska are called "Kodiak bears."

All species of bear living today are threatened with extinction throughout some, if not all, of their range. Sun bears, Asiatic black bears, sloth bears, and spectacled bears are currently classified as "vulnerable" by the World Conservation Union (IUCN), a group made up of governments, scientists, and conservationists from all over the world. This means that these bears face a high risk of extinction in the wild in the medium-term future. The IUCN classifies the polar bear as "lower risk–conservation dependent." This means that if the conservation programs that are in place for polar bears were to stop, these bears would probably qualify as "vulnerable" within five years.

Brown bears and American black bears are not classified by the IUCN, but are considered to be currently threatened with extinction throughout some areas where they

The sloth bear, along with several other bear species, is facing extinction.

Is the Giant Panda a Bear?

The giant panda, which lives in the Sichuan, Shaanxi, and Gansu provinces of China, in the mountain ranges along the eastern side of the Tibetan Plateau, first came to the attention of Western scientists in 1869. Since then, there has been a controversy about whether it is a bear or not. Some scientists argue that the giant panda belongs in the raccoon family, called the Procyonidae, instead of the bear family, called the Ursidae. Some others think it belongs in a family of its own.

Recent genetic studies have implied that the ancestors of the giant panda became distinct from other bears about 20 million years ago, during the Miocene epoch. Since the bear family and the raccoon family are thought to have emerged as separate families earlier than this, these studies suggest that the giant panda is more closely related to bears than to raccoons. Currently the classification of giant pandas as bears is favored, although some contradictory genetic evidence and some differences of opinion within the scientific community still remain.

Giant pandas face problems similar to those faced by bears: declining populations due to habitat destruction and direct killing. Logging and the clearing of bamboo forests for human settlements and agriculture are reducing suitable habitat for giant pandas at the same time that illegal hunting is reducing their numbers. The giant panda is currently considered an endangered species, with an estimated population of only about twelve hundred individuals still living in the wild.

The giant panda lies on the brink of extinction, its numbers dwindling from habitat destruction and hunting.

live. The Louisiana black bear is listed as threatened by the U.S. Fish and Wildlife Service, and the Florida black bear is listed as threatened by the state of Florida. Black bears have already disappeared from some states, including Illinois, Kentucky, and Ohio, and populations in Mexico are thought to be small and shrinking. But in spite of their low populations in some areas, American black bears still have large populations in much of the United States and Canada, and currently exist in greater numbers than any other bear species.

The grizzly bear is listed as threatened by the U.S. Fish and Wildlife Service throughout the contiguous forty-eight states because its population has declined to less than one thousand individuals occupying a few small, isolated areas. The situation is similar in western Europe, where brown bears have suffered extreme population losses, with only tiny populations still surviving in a handful of isolated, mountainous areas. Populations in Asia (with the exception of eastern Siberia) are also small and declining; however, large populations of brown bears still exist in some areas of eastern Europe, Russia, Canada, and Alaska.

Although grizzly bears once could be found throughout most of the contiguous United States, today only about a thousand grizzlies populate this region.

It is difficult to know which bear species is the "most threatened" because many of the species living outside of North America are not well studied and lack reliable population estimates. These little-studied species include sun bears, sloth bears, Asiatic black bears, and spectacled bears. In the case of both the sun bear and spectacled bear, biologists lack such basic information as the size of the range these species need for successful foraging. It is these less-studied bears that are thought to be the most seriously threatened with extinction.

Sun bears (*Helarctos malayanus,* sometimes referred to as *Ursus malayanus*)

Sun bears have been studied the least of all the bears. They live in the rain forests of Southeast Asia, ranging from Burma and Bangladesh, southeast across Laos, Cambodia, Vietnam, and Thailand, and south to the Malay Peninsula and the islands of Sumatra and Borneo. How much of this area they still occupy is not completely known.

Sun bears get their name from the yellowish, orange, or white crescent-shaped mark usually seen on their chests. Other than this colorful mark and the light-colored fur around their muzzles and eyes, these bears are black, with very short, dense fur that repels the moisture of the wet, humid climates where they live. Sun bears have no hair at all on the soles of their feet. Their naked soles and long, curved claws are characteristics that help them climb trees. They are active at night, foraging on a wide variety of foods. These include fruit, honey, earthworms, ants, termites, lizards, birds, and small mammals. Sun bears do not hibernate, which indicates that sufficient quantities of food have traditionally been available to them year-round in their habitats.

Like other Asian species, sun bears face the pressure of a rapidly growing human population as well as the dangers of hunting. Since they are cautious and small, with adult males weighing from 60 to 145 pounds and females even less, they are the least threatening of all the bears. Consequently they are often removed from the wild to be kept as pets and performing animals, which further contributes to their endangerment.

Asiatic black bears (*Selenarctos thibetanus,* sometimes referred to as *Ursus thibetanus*)

The Asiatic black bear usually occupies moist forests in mountainous areas. The species lives in southern Asia, ranging from Pakistan through the Himalaya Mountains of northern India, Nepal, and Bhutan, south to Bangladesh, and continuing eastward into southern China and northern Indochina. It also occurs in northeastern China, Korea, Japan, and eastern Russia. This species is now extinct on

 ### Reproduction
Since each bear in a population needs so much room and so much food, there are not a great many of them in any one area. They produce few offspring, usually two cubs per litter, although the birth of three or even four cubs is not uncommon. The mother takes care of the cubs for one to three years, depending on the species of bear. This extended period of supervision, which includes lessons in foraging as well as protection from predators, increases the chance that each cub will survive to adulthood.

The amount of food a female is able to find has a great effect on how many cubs she will have throughout her lifetime and in any one year's litter, or if she will have any young at all in a particular year. When bears mate, the eggs within the female's body are fertilized but do not implant in her uterus and begin developing for months. Once the eggs have implanted, the young develop quickly, being born within six to eight weeks. However, if the female has not gained enough weight by the time the eggs should implant, implantation does not occur and that female will not have cubs that year.

Bears reproduce slowly. For example, a well-studied population of brown bears on Admiralty Island, Alaska, showed that young females do not begin reproducing until they are about seven years old. They usually have litters only once every four years, and sometimes six years may pass between litters. This means that if a population is to maintain a healthy number of individuals, adult females must live long lives (bears may live for twenty or more years in the wild) and find adequate food so they can produce and successfully raise several litters of cubs.

An Asiatic black bear lies with her four-and-a-half-month-old cubs.

the island of Kyushu in Japan, and only a few individuals remain in Korea. The largest populations of these bears currently occur in eastern Siberia.

Although usually black, Asiatic black bears may also be brown or reddish brown, with lighter fur on their muzzles. They have a broad, V-shaped patch of light fur on their upper chests and often have a mane of long fur on their necks and shoulders. They are fairly large bears, usually weighing between 220 and 440 pounds. Asiatic black bears are primarily vegetarian, but they will also eat ants and insect larvae and hunt both large and small mammals. Their claws aid them in climbing trees, and much of their diet consists of fruits and nuts they find by climbing. In every population studied thus far, these bears have been observed to hibernate. This means that they must store fat during their summer and fall foraging.

Habitat loss has been rapid throughout much of the range of the Asiatic black bear, and forests large enough to sustain healthy populations are becoming less common. Like the sun bear, Asiatic black bears are avidly hunted, and individuals are sometimes removed from the wild to be sold as pets and performing animals.

Sloth bears (*Melursus ursinus,* sometimes referred to as *Ursus ursinus*)

Sloth bears live in India, Sri Lanka, Nepal, Bhutan, and Bangladesh, inhabiting moist evergreen forests, deciduous forests, grasslands, and thorn scrub. When Europeans first encountered and described these bears in the late eighteenth century, they mistakenly believed them to be sloths,

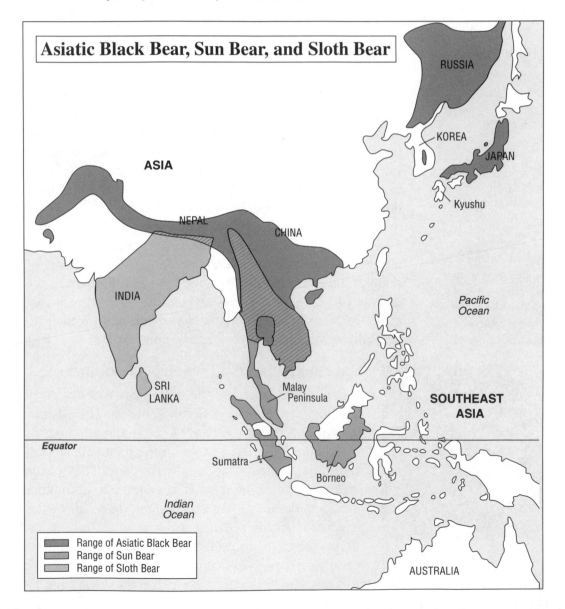

Asiatic Black Bear, Sun Bear, and Sloth Bear

RUSSIA

ASIA

KOREA

JAPAN

Kyushu

NEPAL

CHINA

INDIA

Pacific Ocean

SRI LANKA

Malay Peninsula

SOUTHEAST ASIA

Equator

Sumatra

Borneo

Indian Ocean

Range of Asiatic Black Bear
Range of Sun Bear
Range of Sloth Bear

AUSTRALIA

tree-dwelling mammals that live in the tropics of South and Central America. Sloths often hang upside-down from tree branches, suspended by their long, curved claws. Sloth bears also have long, curved claws, and it was this similarity that led to the initial confusion about their classification. When they were later recognized as bears, the name "sloth bear" endured.

Sloth bears have long, shaggy fur, usually black except for a white blaze on the chest and a white muzzle. They are medium-sized, usually weighing between 175 and 310 pounds. Sloth bears eat mostly termites and ants, using their long, curved claws to dig up and break open termite colonies and their mobile lips and snouts to suck the termites out. They also eat fruit, berries, honey, cultivated sugar cane, corn, and any dead animal matter they are able to find. Their claws aid them in climbing, and they are known to climb and shake fruit trees to secure fruit for themselves. Sloth bears do not hibernate, as food is abundant for them year-round.

The continued existence of these bears is threatened by people moving into their habitat and forested areas being cleared. They appear to be intolerant of the presence of people and may avoid areas disturbed by humans. Like Asiatic black bears and sun bears, sloth bears face heavy pressure from hunting and are sometimes removed from the wild to be trained as performing animals.

Spectacled bears are named for the light markings around their eyes, which make them appear to be wearing glasses.

Spectacled bears (*Tremarctos ornatus*)

Spectacled bears are the only bears that currently occupy the continent of South America. They live in the desert scrub at the base of the Andes Mountains, in the humid tropical forests on the mountain slopes, and in the meadows above the tree line. They occur in and around the mountains of Venezuela, Colombia, Ecuador, Peru, and Bolivia, extending south to the Argentine-Bolivian border.

Spectacled bears get their name from the light markings around their eyes that make them look like they're wearing glasses or spectacles. Other than these light markings, their fur is black and shaggy. They are thought to be active at night. These bears are avid tree climbers and gather food while climbing. Fruit and bromeliads, a family of tropical American plants, are important food sources, with bromeliads making up over half of their diet. Small rodents, birds, insects, and dead animal matter are also eaten by spectacled bears, and they have been known to prey on cattle. Since spectacled bears do not hibernate, they need to find adequate food sources year-round.

Spectacled bears are facing severe habitat loss, particularly in their lower-elevation habitats, and they are avidly hunted as more people move into the areas they occupy. While the number of spectacled bears still in the wild is not known, it is thought to be very low, perhaps less than two thousand individuals.

Polar bears (*Ursus maritimus*)

Polar bears are easily recognized by their large size and white coats. They live in northern Russia, Greenland, Norway, Canada, and Alaska. The area they occupy also includes the oceans that fall between these land masses because they may travel on pieces of floating sea ice.

The polar bear diet consists primarily of ringed seals, but these carnivores also occasionally eat bearded seals, walruses, and small whales, including belugas and narwhals. They often hunt young seals by breaking into the snow lairs that ringed seals occupy during their birthing season. They may also hunt by standing or lying on the ice near the seals' breathing holes; they wait for the seals to surface, then break through the ice and grab their prey. Seals or walruses basking on the ice may also be attacked and eaten by polar bears. Polar bears cover an immense area throughout the year. A bear with a large home range may travel

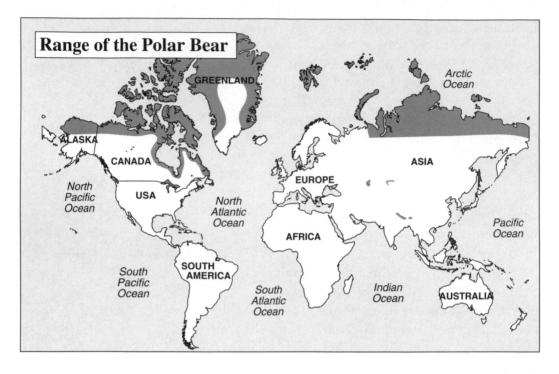

Range of the Polar Bear

more than 135,000 square miles, while a bear with a "small" home range may travel about 20,000 square miles.

In the past, uncontrolled hunting threatened polar bear populations, but currently the largest threat is thought to come from toxins in the environment and global warming. Although an estimated twenty thousand to forty thousand polar bears exist in the wild today, a fairly healthy population, there continues to be concern about the future of this species.

Brown bears (*Ursus arctos*)

The brown bear is the most widespread of all ursine species, occurring in North America, Europe, Asia, and the Middle East. These bears occupy a variety of habitats, ranging from the tundra to deciduous and coniferous forests, grasslands, and desert areas. Between 125,000 and 150,000 brown bears are currently estimated to be in the wild, with about half of these in Russia (especially eastern Siberia) and most of the rest in Canada and Alaska. Brown bear populations in these regions are currently large; however, this bear formerly occupied about twice as much area worldwide as it does today and occurred in much greater numbers than it does now.

The brown bears can be recognized by their large size, the long claws on their front paws, and the prominent hump on their upper backs just over the shoulder area. Despite their name, they are not necessarily brown, but occur in a range of colors including black, cinnamon, and blond. Brown bears use the very long claws on their front paws to dig up tubers, roots, and small burrowing mammals to eat. Their shoulder muscles are extremely well developed to aid them in digging; these bulging muscles form their characteristic hump. Brown bears also eat berries, flowers, grasses, and nuts as well as fish and other aquatic animals, young moose, elk, and decaying animal carcasses. These are large bears, usually weighing between 265 and 975 pounds, and they may need very large areas in which to forage. In some habitats a brown bear will cover up to 500 square miles each year. These bears in northern areas must gain enough weight to prepare for hibernation during the winter months.

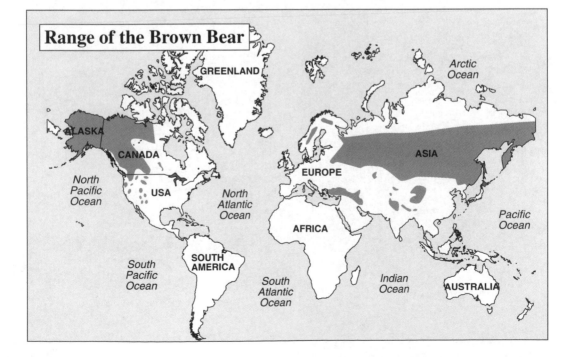

Uncontrolled hunting and habitat loss currently threaten the survival of the brown bear in some regions. Large and powerful, brown bears can be aggressive and dangerous to humans and livestock. In many cases, this has led to their extinction in areas where they have come in contact with people.

American black bears (*Ursus americanus*)

American black bears occur throughout North America. Their range extends from the northern tree limit of the Arctic to central Mexico, and they occupy both deciduous and coniferous forests. An estimated 400,000 to 750,000 American black bears currently exist in the wild, which makes them the most numerous of all the bear species; however, they are disappearing from some of the areas they formerly occupied.

An Alaskan brown bear and its cubs feast on a freshly caught salmon. Brown bears are often mistaken for black bears, although they differ in size.

To the casual eye, American black bears may look very much like brown bears. However, black bears are somewhat smaller, usually weighing between 150 and 500 pounds, with shorter front claws, and lacking the shoulder hump characteristic of the brown bear. Black bears may be black, brown, blond, cinnamon, or even white. They are agile tree climbers and may climb to forage or escape danger. They eat a variety of foods, including berries, grasses, roots, and nuts as well as animal matter such as insects, fish, small mammals, and dead animal carcasses.

The amount of space a black bear needs varies with the area in which it lives, ranging from about sixty square miles for males in some areas to about twenty square miles in others. Throughout many of the regions where they live, these bears hibernate and so must gain massive amounts of weight in the summer and fall. Females of this species are territorial; that is, they defend the areas they occupy and forage in. This behavior probably enhances reproductive success, which is heavily dependent on ample prenatal nutrition. American black bear females also establish territories for their daughters, which may help ensure that they will also be successful in producing cubs.

Black bears are secretive and are generally much less aggressive than brown bears. These characteristics have helped them survive in close proximity to people in many areas; however, they have disappeared from regions of heavy deforestation, and hunting is currently thought to be an increasing threat.

Endangered bears

Many aspects of the lives of bears make them vulnerable to the hazardous effects, both intended and accidental, of human disturbance. Bears need so much food that if their habitat is destroyed or changed they may not get enough to

Hibernation

Bears that live in areas where food is not abundant in the winter go into a state of inactivity called hibernation to conserve energy during this season. Northern populations of the familiar grizzly and American black bears are hibernators, as are female polar bears when they are expecting cubs. During hibernation, the bear retreats into its den, becoming inactive and lethargic. American black bears usually make their dens in a hollow in the earth, in a hollow tree, or in a cave. Grizzly and polar bears usually dig their hibernation dens in the earth or snow. Bears, especially pregnant females, have been noted to select or construct dens in areas that are well concealed and inaccessible to people and other predators.

In his book *The Track of the Grizzly,* biologist Frank Craighead explains that grizzly bears in Yellowstone National Park enter their hibernation dens during snowstorms, making it difficult to follow them to their den sites. He explains, "The grizzlies' habit of entering dens during falling snow served to conceal tracks that might reveal the den locations, to primitive hunters, for instance, and over the ages this could have been a factor favoring grizzly survival."

During hibernation, all of the bear's energy comes from fat stored from foraging the previous spring, summer, and fall. Female polar bears must gain several hundred pounds before hibernating, and American black bears have been observed to spend twenty hours a day foraging in order to build up their fat reserves. A bear that doesn't have enough stored fat will not have enough energy to survive the winter and will die.

Bears that hibernate give birth to their cubs during hibernation. Bear cubs are extremely tiny and hairless at birth and cannot yet maintain a healthy body temperature, so those born in cold climates need the warm, protected environment of the den. The mother usually continues to hibernate for at least several weeks after giving birth, while the cubs feed on milk she produces. Female bears must, therefore, gain enough weight before hibernation to sustain not only themselves, but the developing and nursing cubs as well. Females with dependent cubs hibernate with their cubs; other bears hibernate alone.

eat, resulting in the birth of fewer cubs and the starvation of adults and juveniles alike. As bear habitat disappears and bears wander farther from their traditional ranges looking for food, they are more likely to come in contact with people and be killed. The slow reproduction of bears makes them extremely vulnerable to overhunting. If females are killed before they have a chance to produce several litters and care for those cubs, the number of bears in the population will decline.

2

Habitat Destruction and Protected Lands

PEOPLE HAVE SHARED habitat with bears for thousands of years, with enough resources and habitat available for the continued survival of both. Over the past two hundred years, however, the human population has grown enormously and human technology now allows people to make vast changes to the landscape in extremely short periods of time as they alter the land to better meet their own needs. Thus there is now a risk that people will eliminate bears by consuming the resources bears need for survival.

Habitat fragmentation: a threat to populations

Many populations of bears are isolated in the relatively small wild areas that have remained unspoiled by the dramatic expansion of human development. This separation of habitat into small areas is known as habitat fragmentation, and it threatens the future survival of bears because these remaining islands of habitat are usually too small to support enough bears to make up a self-sustaining population—one that is large and healthy enough to continue existing into the future.

Small populations confined to limited areas are not self-sustaining for two major reasons. The first is that local environmental disasters, such as droughts and fires, which occur from time to time in almost any habitat, are likely to affect an entire population when it is confined to a very small area. Over time, these natural fluctuations in the ability of

27

the area to support bears will drive the population to extinction. The other reason is that small, isolated populations become inbred, so that all the members of the population are closely related and genetically very similar. Often inbred populations produce few young, and these young may not be healthy enough to survive to adulthood; inbred populations may also produce young with physical deformities. These unfavorable results are known as "inbreeding depression," and there is evidence that it can affect small bear populations.

 Female Grizzlies with Cubs Move Away from Males

Female grizzly bears with cubs are more likely than male grizzlies to run into trouble with people. This is because females with cubs aggressively protect their young and also tend to move away from habitat containing male grizzlies, often in the direction of areas occupied by people.

In some species, notably grizzly bears, polar bears, and American black bears, adult males will kill cubs. While the reasons are not well understood, some scientists think that this occurs primarily in populations where new males, not likely to be the father of the cubs, have recently come into the area. Adult females will not mate again until their cubs are ready to be on their own, which usually takes a few years, whereas females that have lost their cubs will be ready to breed again. Thus it may be that adult males can increase their opportunity to mate and father cubs themselves by killing cubs that are not theirs.

However, since there is no direct evidence that male bears can distinguish their own cubs from cubs that are not theirs, the tendency of females with young to avoid adult males remains unexplained.

Female bears that move away from the males' habitat do not always find security. If their new habitat is isolated in a sea of human development, as are many national parks in the United States and Canada, they may forage near human settlements and be killed as "problem bears."

Since bears need so much space and so many resources, they do not usually exist in great numbers even in populations that are large enough to be self-sustaining. In the past, these small numbers caused some scientists to speculate that bear populations might be naturally inbred, and that inbreeding might therefore not have a negative effect on them. However, evidence from Nordic zoos (zoos in Sweden, Denmark, Norway, and Finland) indicates that inbreeding depression can affect bears. Brown bears bred in captivity in Nordic zoos have become inbred because they do not have a wide choice of mates. These bears suffer from small litter sizes and albinism, signs of inbreeding depression. Since populations with these conditions would not be favored for survival in the wild, extensive inbreeding in healthy, self-sustaining wild-bear populations is unlikely. Thus the study results suggest that inbreeding due to habitat fragmentation may lead to inbreeding depression.

How many bears? How many people?

The number of bears necessary for the long-term survival of a population is not absolutely understood. Many biologists who have studied grizzly bears agree that long-term survival in isolated habitats may require a population of one thousand to several thousand bears. In areas where habitat fragmentation has occurred, such as the contiguous United States, such large populations of grizzlies do not exist. The total population of grizzlies in these forty-eight states is probably only about seven hundred to nine hundred bears, and these are divided into six smaller populations. Thus, low population numbers and fragmentation jeopardize their future survival. For some other bears, such as the spectacled bear of South America, the total number of bears still existing in the wild may be only a few thousand, and these are fragmented into several smaller populations, many or all of which may not be large enough to be self-sustaining.

Before the year 1800, there had never been more than about 1 billion people on earth at any one time. More recently, however, modern improvements in health care, nutrition,

*As ever-increasing
amounts of land are
cleared for human use,
bears are left with little
protected territory.*

and sanitation have resulted in a rapid population increase to the current level of 6 billion. The human population continues to grow and some scientists believe there will be about 10 billion people on earth by the year 2025. This growing population changes the landscape by converting it to areas where people can live, shop, travel in cars, grow crops, and graze animals such as cows to be used for human food. Forested habitat is quickly lost and fragmented as land is cleared for agriculture and settlement and the trees themselves are converted to lumber and wood products.

The loss of forested areas

These forests that are being diminished and fragmented serve as home to many species of bear. For example, the sun bear lives in a region of rapid human population growth and is consequently suffering severe habitat loss. Included in its range is Indonesia, which has the fifth-largest human population of any country, with more than 180 million people, and continues to grow rapidly. As cities become overcrowded, urban people move into rural areas, including the rain forests where the sun bear lives. As the people settle and clear the forest, bear habitat is diminished.

In Thailand, another country within the range of the sun bear, most of the population currently lives in rural areas. About 75 percent of the forest cover in this country has been lost since 1945, as forests have been replaced by rubber plantations, oil palm plantations, and rice fields. Other countries in the range of the sun bear have also suffered extreme loss of wildlife habitat, ranging from 41 percent lost in Malaysia and Singapore to 94 percent lost in Bangladesh.

A black bear digs through the garbage of a cabin. Human expansion into forested areas reduces the bears' natural food supply.

Black bears hibernate during the cold winter months. With the loss of their forest habitat, bears have a difficult time finding safe places to hibernate.

The spectacled bear of South America faces similar problems of habitat loss, as poor families move into the Andes Mountains to find land and resources. Once there, people engage in mining, farming, and livestock grazing, activities that change the land and diminish the spectacled bear habitat.

One of the major problems when people move into bear habitat is that food sources are lost. Sun bears, sloth bears, Asiatic black bears, American black bears, and spectacled bears are all dependent on forests for food items, such as fruits, buds, and nuts. In Peru, about 66 percent of spectacled bear habitat has been lost over the past thirty years because the fruits and bromeliads upon which these bears feed have been eliminated.

Loss of forested habitat presents problems other than reduced food supply. Adequate hibernation sites may be scarce when forest cover is depleted, and loss of hibernation sites threatens the survival of cubs. Some recent research suggests that for American black bears living in the seasonally flooded wetlands of the Mississippi floodplain, pregnant females seek dens in the hollows of large forest trees. Such trees offer protection from the flooding, from predators, and from human disturbance. A reduction in the number of large trees reduces the likelihood that females will find denning sites appropriate for successful reproduction.

Loss of forested habitat is a problem for bears even in areas of moderate human population growth. For example, the number of Louisiana black bears has fallen dramatically because timber harvesting and the conversion of forested wetland areas into agricultural land has destroyed 80 percent of the bear's habitat since 1980. In the United States, where the human population is currently growing very slowly, rapid destruction of bear habitat is often triggered by a large demand for resources, such as wood and crops, that can be harvested and sold. Modern farming and logging methods and machinery allow people to change large areas of landscape rapidly and dramatically.

As forests are depleted, bears are pushed into smaller and smaller areas of remaining habitat, which become isolated from other such areas as human expansion and development continue. These small, isolated areas simply cannot support very many bears.

The presence of roads

The presence of roads is another factor that degrades the habitat for bears and results in habitat fragmentation. One problem is that roads may interfere with the movements of bears. For example, highways restrict the movements of grizzlies living in and around Banff National Park in Canada, and may be enough of a barrier to isolate bears in the park from other grizzly bear populations farther south. Genetic research on grizzlies in the Banff area shows that these

A grizzly walks among the tour buses in Alaska. Roads are a threat to all bears and cause many problems for these animals.

bears may be in danger of becoming inbred due to isolation resulting in part from their reluctance to cross highways.

In other cases, grizzlies may travel along small roads that lead them into areas of human development where their presence will not be tolerated. Roads also offer people access to the areas where bears live, increasing the likelihood that bears and people will meet, and that bears will be either killed by cars or shot. Indeed, roadkill is the leading known cause of death for Florida black bears.

Toxins in bear habitat

Polar bears, living at high northern latitudes not heavily occupied or developed by people, are nevertheless at risk from human activities. Toxic chemicals used in industry and insect control are accumulating in the bodies of polar bears, as well as in the bodies of some brown bears and American black bears who feed on contaminated fish.

The poisons discovered in the bodies of polar bears include the insecticides dichlorodiphenyltrichloroethane (DDT) and chlordane, and the toxic industrial chemicals known as polychlorinated biphenyls (PCBs), which were used to make such items as lubricants for industrial machinery, paints, and adhesives. DDT, chlordane, and PCBs cause health problems in humans including birth defects,

A mother polar bear and her cubs swim through the icy waters of their northern habitat. Although polar bear habitats are relatively unharmed by humans, the bears still fall victim to pesticides.

Polar Bears in the Hudson Bay

The polar bears of the western Hudson Bay, a particularly well-studied population, have been getting smaller since the mid-1980s (both lighter in weight and shorter in length). This is especially true of female bears, although males have been affected as well. The number of young who survive their first year of life has also declined. In the early 1980s, 75 percent of polar bear young born in the western Hudson Bay lived through their first year, but today only about half survive. The reasons for this decline in size and survival rate of cubs are not understood, but some conservationists fear that environmental toxins, starvation resulting from global warming, or both may be responsible. In his article "The Polar Bear Slides," Warren Getler quotes the head of research in the toxicology division of the Canadian Wildlife Service, Ross J. Norstrom: "It is unlikely for toxic chemicals alone to be sparking the decline in cub-survival rates. Yet . . . during times of nutritional stress the bears are more likely to suffer from the effects of chemical contaminants."

infertility, and cancer, and have been banned in the United States. However, DDT, chlordane, and PCBs all persist in the environment for long periods of time, and they are still made and used in other countries. Thus they continue to pollute the food chain.

It is thought that DDT, chlordane, and PCBs wind up in Arctic regions because they vaporize in warm climates and are then carried toward the poles by winds. When they reach the cold polar and subpolar regions they condense and settle to earth, where they may enter the food chain through absorption by phytoplankton, the floating plants and plantlike organisms that form the base of the food chain in polar waters. Recent studies show that PCBs and other toxins may also be transported to high northern latitudes by animals, such as salmon, that become contaminated at lower latitudes, then migrate to the northern regions and become part of the food chain there.

DDT, chlordane, and PCBs are stored in the fat of animals, so a fish that eats contaminated phytoplankton will accumulate the toxins in its fat, and the level of toxins will continue to build up as the fish feeds on contaminated food each day. A bear that feeds on contaminated fish ingests the toxins that the fish has accumulated. Thus the bear will inevitably acquire a high concentration of toxins in its body. This process, by which animals at the top of the food chain receive the largest doses of poison, is known as bio-accumulation.

When fat deposits are used up due to starvation, hibernation, or nursing the young, the stored pollutants can be redistributed in the blood to other tissues where they can cause toxic effects. Pollutants consumed by female polar bears are transferred to the young during nursing, which exposes the young to large doses of toxin early in their lives.

Global warming

Warmer temperatures mean less feeding time for polar bears, which use sea ice as a platform from which to hunt seals. When the ice melts and breaks up during the summer, bears often come onto shore and go for months without eating while they wait for the ice to re-form in the fall. Since temperatures in the Arctic have been increasing steadily for the past 150 years, with spring arriving earlier and earlier, polar bears may be enduring longer periods of starvation.

The rise in temperature in the Arctic is part of a global warming trend thought to result from increased levels of carbon dioxide in the atmosphere. Carbon dioxide is released into the atmosphere when fossil fuels, meaning coal, oil, and natural gas, are burned. Human populations burn these fossil fuels to produce energy to power machines such as cars, and for light, heat, air-conditioning, and other conveniences. When carbon dioxide absorbs long-wave radiation given off by the earth, however, the earth's atmosphere gains energy. This energy then contributes to heating the earth in the process known as the "greenhouse effect." Global warming refers to the intensification of the greenhouse effect due to the increased levels of carbon dioxide in the atmosphere.

If warmer temperatures are responsible for the declining condition of polar bears, and if they are part of an ongoing trend of global warming, then polar bear populations may suffer severely in the future, with many bears starving.

Protection in national parks?

One way to preserve unspoiled habitat for bears is to set aside land protected from human development and hunting. In 1872, the United States began a system of national parks with the establishment of Yellowstone National Park. In 1916, the U.S. Congress passed the National Park Service Act, which stated that preservation of wildlife "in such manner and by such means as will leave them unimpaired for the enjoyment of future generations" was one of the goals of the national parks.[4] Today more than 80 million acres of land in the United States are set aside as Park Service land, and other countries have also established national parks and refuges for wildlife.

In many cases national parks and wildlife sanctuaries provide important habitat for bears. For example, Yellowstone National Park and Glacier National Park are among the few areas in the contiguous United States which continue to support grizzly bears. The remote Bukit Baka National Park in the Indonesian state of Kalimantan reports that the sun bear is "common" within the park. Christopher Servheen, who co-chairs the Bear Specialist Group of the World Conservation Union, speculates that the future of the sun bear in Indonesia is "bleak except perhaps in some large national parks."[5] India has established three nature reserves, Ratanmahal, Jessor, and Shoul Paneshwar, specifically for the preservation of sloth bears.

Parks and reserves, however, are often not large enough to support self-sustaining populations of bears and hence cannot be relied on as the sole strategy for conserving bear species. In some cases, the bears do not stay within the park because they need more room. This is especially true of bears with large home-range sizes, such as grizzly bears, polar bears, American black bears, and Asiatic black bears. Since the home-range sizes of other ursine species are not

Brown bears of the Katmai National Park in Alaska. Bears often require more land habitat than the parks can provide, causing the bears to migrate to unprotected regions.

well understood, it is unclear if parks large enough to meet their habitat needs exist. Bears that wander outside the borders of parks lose the protection and remote habitat that the park offers.

The grizzly bears in Banff National Park in Canada need more room than the park provides. Studies of the movements of these bears have shown that they use land both within and outside the park. Effective conservation of these bears would therefore require cooperation between several different land jurisdictions. The problem is further complicated in the case of Banff, and many other parks as well, because areas next to the park are heavily used by people.

There is evidence that the population of sloth bears in Chitwan National Park in Nepal generally stays within the park borders, indicating that this park is large enough to meet their habitat needs. Results from an ongoing study show that these bears need less room to successfully forage than other species of bear. Since they eat mostly termites and ants, foods available throughout the year, sloth bears may not need to make wide movements to find new food sources as the seasons change. This may explain why their home ranges are relatively small. The results of this study have encouraged scientists to think that medium-sized reserves may be large enough to sustain sloth bears. However, it is possible that other sloth bear populations may rely more on other kinds of food, and thus need larger areas in which to forage.

Even if the bears stay within a park or reserve, their survival is not assured. If that park is isolated, the population may lose genetic diversity due to inbreeding. Thus, for yet another reason the protection of isolated parks, though an important part of a larger strategy of conservation, is not a feasible long-term approach to the conservation of bears.

Problems within national parks and reserves

Many national parks in the United States are heavily used by people and crisscrossed with roads, which degrade the habitat for bears. Bears that meet people on trails, at roadsides, and in campgrounds often come to associate people with food and may approach humans, campsites, or cars in search of it. Grizzly bears may also threaten park visitors because they feel that their young or their food sources are at risk. As a result of such encounters, individual animals are often declared "problem bears" and are moved to remote locations or killed in the interest of public safety. Studies with both grizzly bears and American black bears indicate that bears that have been "relocated" (moved to a remote, unpopulated area) often quickly return to the area from which they were moved, and are killed when they resume their "problem" behaviors. Bears moved to a new location often do not survive there.

Bears occupy many campsites and have learned to search for food among human belongings.

Many scientists and conservationists think that the mandate of the U.S. national park system to "provide for the enjoyment of [scenery, natural and historic objects, and wildlife] in such manner and by such means as will leave them unimpaired for the enjoyment of future generations"[6]

Are National Parks for People or for Bears?

As more people come to national parks, encounters between people and bears increase. Most often, the bears quickly turn and flee. In some parks, however, bears have learned to associate people with food, and they may come into camps and rummage through people's belongings in search of it. On rare occasions people have been killed by grizzlies in parks. Some people feel that parks should not allow animals that might injure or kill a person to exist within their borders. However, in more and more areas of the United States and Canada, national parks are the only places where bears can survive. In his article "Homeless on the Range: Grizzlies Struggle for Elbow Room and Survival in Banff National Park," Sid Marty poses the question "if we can't make room for the grizzly bear in the national parks and the lands bordering them, then where can the grizzly, and the wilderness that maintains it, find protection?"

is a paradox because it is almost impossible to provide for people's enjoyment without jeopardizing the continued existence of the objects being enjoyed, including the bears.

National parks and reserves outside the United States also have problems that interfere with their ability to protect bears. In areas such as Southeast Asia where bears are hunted for their body parts, parks and reserves attract poachers, people who hunt or capture animals illegally. Christopher Servheen reports that in one wildlife reserve in Thailand "over 60 well-used poacher camps were found."[7] Some nature reserves in China contain areas where people grow crops. Bears attracted to these crops as a food source are often killed despite laws defining the animals as protected species. And in South America, military activity in national parks has impeded research on spectacled bears. Thus, the manner in which national parks and reserves are used is often not compatible with bear conservation.

3

Hunting and the International Trade

IN THE PAST, the purposeful killing of bears by people severely depleted many bear populations. Today, killing remains a very serious threat to the continued existence of bears. Bears have been, and continue to be, killed for several different reasons. These include hunting for meat, skins, and trophies; hunting so that bear body parts, especially gallbladders, can be used in traditional Asian and South American medicines; hunting to rid areas of dangerous animals; and hunting to protect human agricultural crops and livestock. Bear populations are also threatened by a commercial activity that removes bears from the wild to be used as pets and performing animals.

Bears as trophies, bears as threats

Polar bears are one species whose populations were seriously depleted in the past due to overhunting. Polar bears were heavily hunted so that their body parts, especially their hides, could be displayed or sold as trophies. This hunting continued through the 1960s, with an ever greater toll on polar bear populations as technological advances such as snow vehicles, aircraft, and motorized boats allowed people greater and greater access to the bears. By 1970, the estimated world population of polar bears living in the wild was less than ten thousand. The uncontrolled hunting stopped in 1973, when the nations in which polar bears live all signed the Agreement on Conservation of Polar Bears. This pact, considered a model of international cooperation for the preservation of bears, restricts the places where polar bears can be hunted and the ways in which they can be hunted. In addition, many individual countries have instituted their own, stricter controls on polar bear hunting, or banned it altogether. The increase in the world polar bear population to its current estimate of twenty thousand to forty thousand wild bears is largely attributed to these measures.

Grizzly bears are another species that has been depleted by hunting in some areas. However, their numbers have generally not increased again in those places, even after laws were passed to protect them.

Before the western United States was occupied by settlers of European descent, grizzly bears were widely distributed throughout the west. Now, however, these bears have been hunted to near extinction in the contiguous United States, except for the few remnant populations in Montana, Wyoming, Idaho, and Washington. Unlike polar bears, which were hunted as trophies, grizzly bears were mostly hunted because settlers did not want to coexist with them. Grizzlies were viewed as a threat to human safety and to the livestock and crops of the settlers. Modern firearms made the destruction of grizzly bear populations very effective,

Several bearskins are left to dry in Fairbanks, Alaska. Humans continue to hunt bears for their fur, further depleting the population.

and in the fifty years between 1850 and 1900, the grizzly bear population in the contiguous United States was reduced from about ten thousand to less than one thousand.

Humans are the only natural enemies of grizzly bears, and current efforts to preserve these bears are hampered because people continue to kill them. In general, even in cases where suitable habitat for the bears is available and efforts to increase their numbers have been undertaken, these efforts have not been very successful. Steven Primm of the Northern Rockies Conservation Cooperative points out that "despite dozens of years, millions of dollars, and reams of data that have gone into securing the future of Rocky Mountain grizzly bears . . . their recovery may still be a long way off."[8] In the early 1970s, grizzly bears were listed as a threatened species in the United States under the U.S. Endangered Species Act, and were protected by law. But their killing has continued, largely because the bears exist in close proximity to people and many people view them as competition for resources or as a safety threat. For example, they are sometimes killed by scofflaws who consider them symbols of land use restrictions imposed by the Endangered Species Act. They are also killed by people who fear the bears will damage their crops or livestock. When bears are not tolerated by the local public, laws alone offer relatively little protection.

Even under national protection, grizzlies continue to be threatened by humans.

Studies that have tracked the movements of bears in the Rocky Mountains indicate that more than 85 percent of all adult and weaned juvenile grizzly bears ended up being killed by people. In many cases, the killing of grizzlies is prompted when the bears wander into territory occupied by people, such as towns, campgrounds, and grazing areas for livestock. Studies on grizzly bears at Banff National

 ## How Many Bears Are There?

Since bears often live in forested areas, with individuals spread out over large distances, it can be very difficult to observe them and adequately estimate the size of a population. This means that it is often not easy to figure out whether the number of bears in an area is increasing, decreasing, or remaining about the same, and misperceptions about numbers can easily go unnoticed for some time.

Better methods for estimating bear numbers rely on the observations of trained biologists or wildlife staff. When making observations, scientists may systematically travel through forests and mountains in the spring looking for bear prints in the snow or mud, or they may capture bears and mark them in some way so that the animals can be recognized. This allows researchers to tell when they see a bear whether they have seen it before or whether it is a new observation.

Knowledge of bear biology also helps scientists in estimating population size. For example, people who see more bears on their property during a summer than ever before may conclude that the number of bears in the population is increasing. Specialists familiar with area conditions and bear behavior might point out that bears are coming out of the forest in search of food in response to drought conditions.

Adequately assessing the number of bears in a population is important when it comes to making decisions about whether hunting needs to be controlled to protect the bears. Failure to accurately assess the number of bears can place the bear population at risk because an underestimate may result in a decision not to institute the legal protection necessary for their survival.

Park in Canada indicate that there are probably only about sixty to eighty grizzlies currently living in and around the park. An additional seventy-three bears died near Banff between 1971 and 1995; fifty-two of these bears died after being relocated or were killed because they were considered a threat to the public. Almost all the bears that were killed died near areas of human development.

Bears and human settlements

Bears are flexible about what they will eat, and they readily turn to crops, livestock, and even human garbage as food sources, especially when their traditional foods become scarce due to habitat destruction. Grizzly bears are not the only bears that are killed because people see them as competitors for resources; American black bears, which frequently raid human trash and campsites in search of food, are at risk as well. In areas such as Southeast Asia and the Andes Mountains of South America, where people are currently moving into bear habitat, bears are killed as pests, much as the grizzly bears were killed in the western United States in the nineteenth century. Killings persist even in areas where laws exist to protect bears.

Besides grizzlies, bears currently killed as agricultural pests include sun bears, Asiatic black bears, and spectacled bears. Sun bears will attack livestock and feed on fruits grown for human use, like bananas and papayas. They will also eat the heart of the cultivated oil palm tree, thereby killing the tree. Asiatic black bears in China are known to raid crops such as corn and to attack livestock. In Japan, Asiatic black bears have turned to plantations of cedar and cypress, feeding on these trees by tearing the bark off and eating the cambium underneath. The cambium is a layer where new, living cells and their nutritious contents are synthesized. It is also a comparatively soft layer, easier to chew than mature wood. Spectacled bears of South America raid cornfields and attack livestock in the farms and pastures of the Andes Mountains.

Sometimes bears will also turn to eating human garbage or will seek human food even when natural food sources

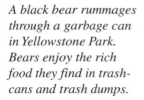

A black bear rummages through a garbage can in Yellowstone Park. Bears enjoy the rich food they find in trash-cans and trash dumps.

appear to be readily available. Human garbage and human foods are rich food sources for bears, since both bears and people tend to prefer foods high in nutrition and fat. For example, before 1970, Yellowstone National Park had open-pit dumps for the garbage produced by visitors to the park. Grizzly bears gathered at these dumps to feed. The richness of this garbage as a food source is apparent because several bears regularly congregated at the dumps to eat.

Bears tend to avoid each other when foraging in areas where food is limited. In fact, some scientists believe that the solitary behavior of bears may have evolved because a single concentrated area seldom offers enough food to support a group of these animals. Thus the chances of obtaining an adequate amount of food are usually greater for a bear foraging alone.

Hunting for bear body parts

In addition to being hunted as trophies, dangerous predators, and competitors for resources, all bear species are presently also heavily hunted for their body parts, which are used by individuals or sold commercially for medicinal purposes. The practice of hunting bears for body parts is currently so intense that it is considered as large a threat to their continued survival as the destruction of their habitat.

Asian traditional medicine calls for the use of bear gallbladders, meat, brains, blood, bones, paws, and spinal cords as ingredients in medications. Bear fat, meat, and paws are often used as foods that are thought to impart medicinal benefits to those who consume them. For example, according to Chinese tradition, eating bear paw stew strengthens the body and prevents colds. Spectacled bear body parts are also used in traditional folk medicines in the Andes of South America. For example, the fat of spectacled bears is believed to assist in the healing of bone bruises, the treatment of rheumatism, the alleviation of muscle pain, and the curing of blindness; the gallbladders of all bear species are considered a cure for blindness and

 ## Will People Tolerate the Threat Bears Pose?

Like other large predators, bears can be dangerous to people and livestock. In a draft statement issued by the U.S. Fish and Wildlife Service, officials speculated that if grizzly bears were reintroduced to the Bitterroot ecosystem in Montana and Idaho, and a population of approximately three hundred individual bears established there, the "grizzly bear population would kill about 6 cattle (4–7), [and] 22 sheep (0–44) . . . per year. . . . Nuisance bear incidents could be up to 59 (0–118) per year. . . . Risk to human health and safety from a recovered grizzly bear population would be less than 1 injury per year and less than 1 human mortality every few decades." As many biologists and conservationists have pointed out, the recovery of bear populations cannot be successful unless people who encounter and live with the bears are tolerant of their presence, which includes being willing to incur some risk, even if it is slight, to their own safety and that of their livestock and other property.

In an article entitled "A Global Perspective on Large Carnivore Conservation," William Weber and Alan Rabinowitz observe that North Americans are not as tolerant of the presence of large predators as are people on other continents: "Asians, Africans, and Latin Americans are living with tigers, leopards and jaguars in their backyards, whereas North Americans resist the return of the wolf to our most remote regions and call for renewed hunting of mountain lions in California." They suggest that such widespread rejection of risk may result in "the continued decline and ultimate disappearance of many of the world's most spectacular large carnivores."

cataracts in many parts of the world. Spectacled bear parts are also said to have magical properties. Thus, the bones are ground up and eaten to impart strength, and the claws and baculi (plural of baculus, a bone found in the ursine penis) are used as amulets to impart strength and fertility to people.

Bear gallbladders are especially sought after in Asia, and the bile salts found within them are highly prized in Asian folk medicines. These salts are usually taken in a dried, crystalline form. In China they are used to treat such serious ailments as liver disease, burns, high blood pressure, jaundice, heart disease, and diabetes. In Korean traditional medicine they are used to alleviate digestive problems and inflammation and to "purify the blood." Although bear bile salts have been used for centuries in these medicines, the hunting pressure on bears is particularly intense now for several reasons: human populations are large, habitat destruction gives people greater access to bears, modern firearms make bear hunting easier and more efficient, and modern transportation allows extensive trade. Judy A. Mills, a contributor to the book *Bears: Majestic Creatures*

Humans continue to buy bear body parts as souvenirs and for use in traditional medicines. The massive claws of bears are thought to endow people with strength and fertility.

of the Wild, states that "there are fewer than one million bears on Earth and more than one billion potential consumers of bear parts as medicine."[9]

Clinical tests have shown that ursodeoxycholic acid (UDCA), the active ingredient in bear bile, does have medicinal properties. Western doctors are currently using UDCA to dissolve gallstones. Trials of its effectiveness in treating cirrhosis of the liver, hepatitis, and blood cholesterol problems are currently being undertaken in the West as well. Bears are not the only animals to have UDCA in their bile salts. Other mammals have it as well, but bears are the only animals that have significant quantities of it. However, the amount of UDCA found in bear gallbladders varies considerably from bear to bear, suggesting that bear gallbladders are not a guaranteed source for UDCA.

UDCA can be synthesized from cow bile in the laboratory, and it is this synthesized UDCA that Western doctors are using in medicines. It appears to have all the medicinal properties of bile taken from the gallbladders of bears and it is inexpensive. However, the teachings of Asian medicine hold that the bile salts from wild bears are more effective than synthetic UDCA and more easily assimilated by the human body. Thus, the hunting continues.

International trade in bear body parts

Large amounts of money can be made from selling the body parts of bears, especially the gallbladders. The prices paid for gallbladder vary significantly, with sales in Asia in the early 1990s ranging from $1 to $210 per gram. Sometimes significantly more money can be made. For example, the gallbladder of an Asiatic black bear illegally killed in South Korea sold at a public auction for $64,000. The World Wide Fund for Nature (WWF) points out that on a price-per-gram basis, bear gallbladders often cost more than gold. This makes bears very attractive targets for poachers. Judy A. Mills, in *Bears: Majestic Creatures of the Wild,* points out just how attractive trade in bear parts can be when she states, "Selling a single bear, or a bear gallbladder, can at least double a person's annual income in many Asian countries."[10]

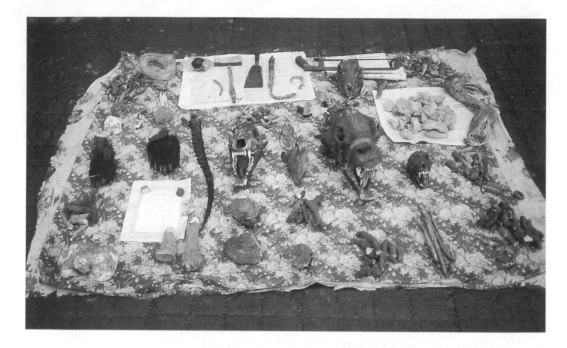

Animal parts are sold in China. The selling of bear body parts has become a large market in many Asian countries.

Since bear parts can be sold for so much money and since bears are becoming scarcer and scarcer in many Asian countries, a large and mostly illegal market in international trade has become established. Since Asiatic black bears, the only bears native to South Korea, are now extremely scarce in that country, bears from other countries are imported to South Korea for use in medicines. Many of these bears appear to come from Japan, where bear gallbladders are used in *kampoyaku,* the traditional medicine of that country. So many of Japan's Asiatic black bears are exported to South Korea, however, that Japan imports gallbladders from other countries to meet its own domestic needs. Markets for imported bear parts and gallbladders appear to be centered in South Korea, China, Japan, Hong Kong, and Taiwan as well as in Asian communities in the United States and Canada.

As Asian bear populations shrink to very low numbers, bears from other parts of the world are expected to be impacted by hunting for body parts. It is thought that bear parts are beginning to be imported in Asia from North America, where the American black bear is abundant.

Wildlife law enforcement agencies have discovered that poaching of American black bears for their gallbladders and other parts is being practiced in the United States and Canada, and is thought to be fairly widespread throughout these two countries. WWF reports that the American black bear is now heavily impacted by the illegal trade in wildlife parts and says that North American bear parts and entire carcasses have been discovered being imported to Korea, Japan, and Taiwan. WWF fears that in the absence of effective intervention, the American black bear will be pushed toward extinction by the trade in its parts.

CITES: The Convention on International Trade in Endangered Species of Wild Fauna and Flora

The Convention on International Trade in Endangered Species of Wild Fauna and Flora (CITES) is an international agreement that controls trade in endangered and threatened species. The first countries signed the agreement in 1975; it has since been signed by most of the countries that frequently trade wildlife.

When nations sign the CITES they agree not to trade species that are considered to be endangered, except for the beneficial purposes of scientific research or display (in a zoo, for example). Species considered "endangered" are listed in Appendix I of the CITES. The bears listed in Appendix I are the sloth bear, the sun bear, the Asiatic black bear, the brown bear, and the spectacled bear. Species not currently considered endangered, but thought to need monitoring because they may be at risk of becoming endangered, are listed in Appendix II of the CITES. The bears listed in Appendix II are the American black bear and the polar bear.

The CITES is a voluntary agreement between the countries that sign it. It is up to each individual country to enforce its provisions by making sure that the species listed in the appendices are traded only according to the rules set out by the agreement. The CITES is concerned only with trade *between* countries, not with trade *within* a country.

Bears as Pets and Performers

Bears are sometimes taken from the wild to be kept as pets or trained and used as performing animals. Since only very young bears can be trained, cubs are taken from their mothers and raised by people. This depletes wild populations not only because cubs are being removed from the wild, but because the mother bear is usually killed as well. For every female whose reproductive life is cut short, a population experiences a drop in the number of young produced.

Bear cubs, especially sun bears and Asiatic black bears, can sometimes be purchased as pets at markets in Asia. New owners may care for the cubs like puppies, but as the juvenile animals grow and become more difficult to deal with, many are sold to be used for food and a source of body parts. Interestingly, some bears sold as pets do not share this fate. Buddhists in Thailand, who believe that taking care of wild animals earns merit in the afterlife, often buy bear cubs and raise them as honored pets. Judy A. Mills describes the life of some of these bears in *Bears: Majestic Creatures of the Wild:* "Some pet bears in Thailand enjoy daily baths, blankets on chilly nights, taxi rides cross-country and fruit peeled for their pleasure. One beloved Asiatic black bear received a full Buddhist funeral upon his death."

Bears have served as human entertainment for many years. Here a gypsy walks with his three-year-old dancing bear named "Mercan."

However, many countries also have laws and/or agreements to restrict killing and trading of bears and bear parts *within* their borders.

In spite of the CITES agreement, the international trade in bear parts appears to be a booming business and those trading bear parts have devised many ways around the regulations. For example, it is difficult to tell bear gallbladders from those of many other mammals, and dishonest dealers sometimes ship bear organs labeled as being from pigs. Before American black bears were added to Appendix II of the CITES in 1992, gallbladders taken from Asian species were often purposely mislabeled as American black bear gallbladders. Now all bears are listed, but the CITES is set up in a way that allows any nation to take an animal off the list or simply to neglect to enforce the measures for a given species. For example, Japan removed the Asiatic black bear from the Japanese CITES list because of the bear's economic trade importance.

The CITES is just one aspect of a much wider effort to preserve threatened and endangered species. It is designed to work in concert with education programs and captive breeding programs. Provision to allow international trade in endangered species for captive breeding and education will remain in effect as long as such trade is used to benefit the survival of the species. Bears are currently being captive-bred in zoos for conservation purposes, and these animals may travel between countries as they are paired with appropriate mates.

4

Captivity and Reintroduction

Many zoos house endangered and threatened species in their exhibits, both maintaining and breeding them in captivity. As wild populations of many animals have begun to decline, and as habitat has shrunk and become fragmented, zoos have started to see their mission as the conservation of animals that might otherwise become extinct. The Species Survival Plan is an international effort among zoos, sponsored by the American Zoo and Aquarium Association (AZA). The goal of the Species Survival Plan is to ensure that populations of selected species maintain enough genetic variability to continue to exist into the future. The bears that are currently part of the Species Survival Plan are the spectacled bear, the sun bear, and the sloth bear.

Species Survival Plan

Members of the species named in the AZA plan are currently captive-bred in zoos, and such breeding may have the potential to help preserve bears in the wild. Keeping and breeding animals in places other than their natural habitat is referred to as *ex situ* (off-site) preservation. The presence of "off-site" bears in zoos ensures that individuals of the species will continue to exist in the foreseeable future regardless of what happens to wild populations. However, the major goal of captive maintenance is to help preserve populations in the wild. Thus *ex situ* bears might be introduced into wild populations that are losing genetic diversity as a result of their small size or their isolation. By promoting genetic variability, such introductions could help prevent the conditions that can lead to inbreeding depression in wild populations. There is, of course, the danger that the captive-bred bear populations in zoos will themselves become inbred, as happened with the brown bears in Nordic zoos (described in Chapter 2).

In an attempt to prevent inbreeding of captive populations, international studbooks have been established. These books contain records of all the animals of a single species that are held in captivity, including pedigree information for each animal, tracing their ancestry as far back as possible. These studbooks are used by zoos in order to find suitable mates for the animals in their collections. By using studbooks, bears of the same species that are not closely related can be identified and bred. A studbook for the spectacled bear has been established and these bears have been actively bred in captivity with its use since the 1970s. The spectacled bear studbook is published annually and contains management articles and a bibliography of literature about the species, as well as information about the individual captive bears. With the help of captive breeding, the number of spectacled bears in zoos has increased from 44 in 1962 to 175 in 1992, with only 50 of the 175 having been

 Can Zoos Help Wild Bear Populations?
Fred W. Allendorf of the University of Montana, a contributor to *Principles of Conservation Biology,* by Gary K. Meffe, C. Ronald Carroll, and others, reports that he and a colleague developed a computer model to help them estimate how quickly an isolated grizzly bear population of a given size will lose its genetic variation due to inbreeding. This model predicted that introducing just two unrelated bears into an isolated population of grizzlies every generation would greatly slow the rate at which genetic variation would be lost. He suggested that, in some cases, individuals bred in zoos could be introduced into wild populations as a source of new genes. His results indicated that *ex situ* preservation may ultimately be necessary if we are to preserve populations of bears living on isolated nature reserves.

born in the wild. Sun bears and sloth bears have only recently become a part of the Species Survival Plan; both species were added in 1994.

In addition to *ex situ* conservation of species, the Species Survival Plan includes *in situ* (on-site) conservation, which are efforts to preserve wild habitat and to support field research on wild populations. For example, the Bear Advisory Group of the AZA has recommended that the AZA and the World Conservation Union (IUCN) work together to establish an on-site conservation program for sun bears.

Zoos: schools for people, prisons for bears?

The role of zoos as education centers for the public is considered to be vital to the preservation of species. Member organizations of the IUCN point out that massive numbers of people come to zoos, with about 600 million people visiting zoos worldwide each year. This makes zoos a good place to educate the public about the importance of maintaining biodiversity in nature. Zoos house popular and attractive species, such as polar bears and giant pandas, and people's interest in learning about species preservation may be stimulated by these charismatic animals.

A grizzly bear extends a paw outside his cage at the Baltimore Zoo. Zoos educate humans about bears and many other wild animals.

There is general agreement among biologists and conservationists that for the conservation of bears to be successful, the public must perceive this goal as worthwhile. Assuming that people are more likely to value what they understand, education in zoos could make a contribution to the development of more-positive attitudes. This might then translate into public support for laws protecting bears and their habitat, and support for conservation projects, such as the reintroduction of bears into wild areas.

Bears are large animals, and individuals in the wild spend much of their time foraging. Brown bears in Europe have been discovered to spend 45 to 60 percent of the day and night searching for food. When gathering food in the wild, they rely on their memory, experience, and curiosity as well as their senses, especially their sense of smell. The behaviors involved in foraging are complex, and the bear directs much of its energy toward them. Bears in zoos do not usually have the opportunity to use these foraging behaviors and certainly do not have the space to establish a normal foraging pattern. Zoo bears are often kept in barren concrete pits, an environment that offers nothing to investigate. In addition, bears in captivity traditionally are given one daily meal presented to them directly; thus they do not have to use any complex behaviors to locate or secure the food, and they can consume it in an extremely short period of time. In these captive conditions bears often develop abnormal behaviors, such as incessantly pacing back and forth in their enclosures, for lack of an opportunity to direct their behavior toward a biologically meaningful activity. These abnormal behaviors are called "stereotypies."

Research recently initiated in zoos shows that abnormal behaviors in captive bear populations can be reduced if the bears are fed in such a way that requires them to use investigatory behaviors to secure their meals. One method that has been found to be effective is to hide food throughout the enclosure, so that bears need to spend time finding it and figuring out how to obtain it from many different sites. As more zoos adopt feeding methods that encourage naturalistic behavior in bears, the welfare of captive bear populations will no doubt be improved.

Bear farming in China and Korea

In China, and North and South Korea, Asiatic black bears and brown bears are bred and kept in captivity so that bile from their gallbladders can be extracted for use in medicinal preparations. The extraction of the bile is referred to as "milking." The bile is removed from the live animal through a catheter surgically implanted into the gallbladder. Keeping bears for this purpose is called "bear farming," and currently about eight thousand bears live on such farms in China.

The Future of Bears in Zoos

As part of the effort to convert today's zoos into centers for the preservation of biodiversity, the AZA recommends that zoos allot more space for the housing of animals involved in the Species Survival Plan. For example, Asiatic black bears have not been included in the plan, in part because so few are in captivity in North America that it was judged impractical to successfully breed them for healthy genetic variability. Thus the AZA has suggested that when Asiatic black bears die or are sent to other zoos, their spaces be filled with bears involved in the plan. Space occupied by American black bears, which are still abundant throughout much of their range, is similarly slated to go to bears involved in the Species Survival Plan.

Bear farming has been presented as a means of obtaining the bile salts that are in such high demand in Asian countries, without turning to wild bears as a source. Bear farming also guarantees a supply of bile for use in medicines. As wild bears become scarcer, an ensured supply may be important for the demand for bear bile to be met. Largely because of the belief held by many consumers that the bile of a wild bear is more effective than the bile of a captive specimen, however, bear farming does not appear to have stopped or slowed the demand for bile from wild bears.

Bears wearing catheters for bile extraction are apparently not in pain. However, they are usually kept in very small cages throughout their lives. Under wild conditions bears move through large home ranges and spend many hours of the day searching for food and eating. Bears kept in tiny cages on bile farms probably experience considerable stress and an extremely low quality of life.

Reintroduction of bears into the wild

One of the main objectives of the captive breeding of bears in zoos is the possibility of reintroducing bears into the wild. Many scientists believe that if all seven species of bear are to ultimately continue to exist in the wild, such reintroductions will be necessary. Past experiences show that this method can be effective in repopulating areas from which bears have been eradicated but which still offer high-quality bear habitat. Thus far, however, bears introduced in such areas have usually been animals caught in the wild from other areas, as opposed to animals bred in captivity.

A program aimed at black bears in Arkansas is considered one of the most successful reintroductions of a large carnivore ever. It began in 1958, at which point black bears had been extinct in Arkansas for almost forty years due to a combination of overhunting and habitat destruction. About 250 bears, wild-caught in Minnesota and Manitoba, Canada, were introduced to remote areas in the Ozark and Ouachita Mountains over a period of eleven years. Kimberly G. Smith, Joseph D. Clark, and Scott D. Shull, contributors to *Bears: Majestic Creatures of the Wild,* edited by Ian Stirling, describe the reintroduction:

Reintroducing bears to areas where large numbers of the species once thrived allows their population to recover.

The animals were transported to Arkansas in pickup trucks, each of which accommodated six bears in individual cages. Release areas were chosen for their remoteness and the availability of food and water. Feeding troughs of dog food were placed at the release sites, so the bears would not go hungry while learning about their new home, and the food was eaten by some of the bears.[11]

In 1988, twenty years after the reintroductions ceased, the Arkansas Game and Fish Commission estimated that there were about twenty-one hundred black bears living in the Ozark and Ouachita Mountains, indicating that the bears were reproducing very successfully in the area.

The experience in Arkansas was successful probably because a relatively large number of bears were released each year, a lot of high-quality habitat was available, and the release sites were far from centers of human population. These criteria are now thought to be essential for the successful recolonization of an area by bears. Another factor that might have aided in the success of this effort was the fact that the relocated bears were not captive-bred and thus already knew how to survive in wild situations.

At least two European countries have experimented with the reintroduction of captive-bred brown bears: Romania and Bulgaria. In Romania, the brown bear population had dropped to an estimated one thousand bears by 1950. In

The process of trapping bears in highly populated habitats and then reintroducing them to less populated areas has been practiced by many nations in an effort to increase bear populations.

Western Europe Reintroduces Brown Bears

Many countries in western Europe are currently working to enlarge their remaining brown bear populations by introducing bears from eastern Europe. WWF is involved in assisting France, Italy, and Austria in their efforts to increase the number of brown bears within their borders. The French government has prohibited hunting of the tiny population of brown bears still existing in the Pyrenees Mountains, closed the roads leading to the bears' habitat, and requested that Slovenia send bears to France for introduction into these mountains. Italy is also considering the introduction of bears from Slovenia and Croatia into the Italian Alps, where as few as five brown bears may currently live. Austria has already introduced two brown bears from the former Yugoslavia and has plans to introduce more brown bears in the future. It is too early to measure the success of these efforts.

an attempt to increase the number of bears in the country, limits were imposed on hunting, and the Forest Administration released over 300 captive-born bears into such high-quality habitat areas as the Carpathian Mountains. As a result of these efforts, the number of brown bears in Romania had increased to six thousand by 1990. The Bulgarian program also entailed the release of captive-bred brown bears into the wild (in this case, the central Balkan Mountains) for the purpose of hunting.

From a biological perspective it is obviously possible to reintroduce bears into the wild successfully. However, the question of whether people will tolerate the reintroduced populations is of real concern. The successful reintroduction of black bears into Arkansas was done without publicity and without informing the local public that bears were being brought in. In fact, now that the number of bears in Arkansas is high, the number of complaints about bears is also high, although recent surveys suggest that Arkansas landowners are somewhat positive in their response to the reintroduction program.

Reintroduction of grizzlies into the Bitterroot ecosystem

The U.S. Fish and Wildlife Service is currently proposing to reintroduce wild grizzly bears from other areas into the Bitterroot ecosystem of Idaho and Montana. Grizzly bears formerly occupied this ecosystem, which comprises the largest tract of wild mountain habitat remaining in the United States today, but no grizzlies or their footprints have been seen there since the 1940s. When the grizzly bear was first added to the list of threatened species under the U.S. Endangered Species Act in 1975, the Bitterroot ecosystem was recognized as a good, remote habitat where relocated grizzlies might be successful enough that their population would grow and thus recover from its threatened status.

In an attempt to win public support for the grizzly reintroduction, the Fish and Wildlife Service is proposing that the bears be designated as a "non-essential, experimental population." This category allowed by the Endangered Species Act means that the bears would not be granted all the protections that a threatened species is usually granted. Decisions that might impact the bears—like whether a portion of national forest in which the bears were living could be logged, or whether a bear killing livestock could be shot—would be made by a committee of citizens, bypassing the machinery authorized under the Endangered Species Act. In fact, the plan that the Fish and Wildlife Service is proposing for this reintroduction is supported by logging companies in the area because they do not want the bears reintroduced with the full protection of the Endangered Species Act, in case this would hinder their ability to cut trees in the area.

In spite of efforts by the Fish and Wildlife Service to respond to the concerns of the citizens of Idaho and Montana, the governor of Idaho, Phil Batt, wrote to Secretary of the Interior Bruce Babbitt about the proposed reintroduction, stating that "reintroduction will pose a significant safety risk for Idaho's citizens, and many tourists who visit

"An animal rights advocate was here today, asking questions...I ate him!"

our wilderness areas."[12] Other politicians from Idaho and Montana have also indicated that they do not support the plan to introduce grizzly bears to the Bitterroot ecosystem. However, polls of local residents of the area indicate that about 64 percent support the reintroduction under the "non-essential, experimental" status. Poll respondents cited personal safety as their largest concern regarding the reintroduction.

Some biologists and conservationists see this reintroduction plan as not affording enough protection to the bears to ensure that the reintroduced population will survive. Bears were eradicated from the area in the first place due to overhunting and habitat encroachment, and under the proposed plan these could legally continue to go on. Fears about the success of the proposed grizzly reintroduction echo the problems faced by bears worldwide. Without human tolerance and a commitment to land use practices that are consistent with maintaining high-quality habitat for bears, the number of wild bears will continue to decline no matter how advanced our knowledge about their needs becomes and no matter how successful we are at breeding them in captivity.

5

The Future
of the Bear

IF THE DELIBERATE killing of bears and the destruction of their habitat continue as at present, many bear species will cease to exist outside of zoos and a few protected wild areas. Such remnant populations are likely to be small and isolated and thus in danger of being driven to extinction as a result of inbreeding, local environmental disasters, or both.

For bear conservation to be successful, populations that can sustain themselves far into the future need to be established. There are several different ways that this could be achieved. One way would be to set aside habitat large enough to maintain a self-sustaining population of bears, and then protect the bears within this habitat. However, since most bears need very large territories in which to roam, it may not be practical to set aside an area of habitat large enough to maintain a healthy population of bears.

Habitat corridors

Another way to establish self-sustaining bear populations is to join patches of habitat together by creating corridors, or passageways, of protected habitat between them. Individuals could travel along these corridors to disperse into other populations and breed with the bears there, introducing new genetic material.

One of the most attractive features of habitat corridors is that they would greatly reduce the size of the area needed to sustain a healthy population of bears. For example, in the northern Rocky Mountains, 80,419 square miles of habitat is thought to be necessary to sustain a population of five hundred grizzly bears. Unfortunately, no wilderness area or park existing in North America today is this large. However, if corridors were established between smaller wild areas, a large area would effectively be created by the joining of the small ones.

Since bears often travel long distances, scientists believe that individuals would indeed move from population to population if corridors were provided. However, there is concern that only male bears might travel the long distances required to connect patches of habitat. Females tend to cover less territory, making them less likely to move between widely separated populations. Another potential concern is the presence of roads. The refusal of female grizzly bears in Canada's Banff National Park to cross highways isolates them from other bears. Female grizzlies in Banff will not even use highway underpasses built for wildlife crossing.

Grizzly bears need large areas of habitat to survive. The creation of habitat corridors may help increase these bears' living space.

Habitat Corridors for Giant Pandas

The Management Plan for the Giant Panda, designed by the WWF and the Chinese Ministry of Forestry, was recently approved by China's State Council. This plan calls for the establishment of fourteen new reserves for the giant panda, in addition to the thirteen that already exist. An important aspect of the plan is the creation of habitat corridors consisting of bamboo forest between reserves. These corridors would connect fragmented panda populations, allowing them to move back and forth and interbreed. Estimates of the cost to make this plan a reality run as high as $100 million.

The Chinese government and the WWF have invested tremendous resources into the preservation of the giant panda. Most species of bear lack such support from the governments of the countries in which they live, and from the general public. But conservationists will closely watch the effects of habitat corridors for giant pandas to evaluate this strategy for other populations threatened by fragmented and isolated habitats.

If a successful network of corridors is to be established, these problems will have to be resolved. Some strides toward setting up habitat corridors have been made. For example, in Banff, plans to remove an airstrip and army camp that interfere with wildlife movements have been announced.

Moving bears from population to population

Another option for establishing self-sustaining bear populations is for people to periodically move a few bears from one population and release them into another. This would help prevent inbreeding even without habitat corridors. Some scientists think that genetic variability could also be maintained in an isolated bear population if a few captive-bred bears were periodically released into it. This is a possibility for bears included in the Species Survival Plan or bears that are part of a large captive population.

In habitat areas rich enough to support many more bears than currently exist there, several individuals could be introduced to enlarge the population. Indeed, periodically moving American black bears or European brown bears from population to population may be feasible. For sun bears, spectacled bears, and sloth bears, however, such transfers probably could not be done without endangering the population from which the bears were taken. Even the proposed reintroduction of grizzly bears into the Bitterroot ecosystem has been challenged by some conservation organizations; they believe the areas that the Fish and Wildlife Service proposes to raid do not have large enough populations to sustain the loss.

Reducing human-bear conflict

All the strategies for establishing self-sustaining populations of bears will fail if hunting goes unchecked. Preventing overhunting is likely to require laws that effectively protect bears everywhere. In many areas, current laws are ineffective because they are not enforced. For example, all the countries in South America that have spectacled bears now have protective laws. However, little money is allocated to hire and train people to enforce these laws. As a result, spectacled bears continue to be killed, often by cattle ranchers who fear for their livestock. If laws protecting bears are to be effective, not only must they be strictly enforced, but the conservation effort must be supported by the local people who come in contact with bears. This means that bears' human neighbors need to view them as worth preserving instead of seeing them only as competitors for resources. In an article entitled "Human Culture and Large Carnivore Conservation in North America," Yale University's Stephen R. Kellert and his colleagues at Memorial University of Newfoundland point out that "the success of efforts to conserve grizzly bears . . . will depend as much on social acceptance by the regional public as on biological variables."[13]

In attempts to promote harmony between bears and ranchers, compensation programs have been instituted in

"Just what were you planning on doing in the woods?"

some areas to pay ranchers for livestock killed by bears. Another way to keep bears out of areas where they may be killed by people is to fence off the areas where bears will not be tolerated. For example, in Austria, solar-powered electric fences have been installed to protect farms of honeybees from brown bears. Recently the Minister of Canadian Heritage announced that the town of Banff, near Banff National Park, will be fenced as will some campgrounds, in order to reduce human-bear conflict.

Ecotourism

In some cases, bears actually increase the economic well-being of the local people and are therefore tolerated. In certain areas, "ecotourism" has become an economic incentive for people to conserve wildlands and wildlife. Tourists coming to view the wildlife or wildlands make these ecological features an economic asset to the area.

Some areas inhabited by grizzly bears and polar bears are magnets for ecotourists. For example, the town of Churchill, in Manitoba, Canada, is referred to as "the polar bear capital of the world." Thousands of ecotourists come to this town on the western Hudson Bay every year to see the polar bears from the windows of "tundra buggies," which transport people to the areas where the bears congregate. This ecotourism brings millions of dollars to the town every year.

Although polar bears congregate near the town of Churchill while they are waiting for the sea ice to refreeze, and grizzly bears congregate in some areas where rich food sources, especially salmon, are abundant, bears usually live spread far apart, and those that dwell in the forest are difficult to see. Currently, ecotourism to view bears is not a large industry except in some areas of Canada and Alaska. There is some fear that the development of tourism could have a negative effect, because the building of hotels and restaurants to serve visitors may degrade the quality of the habitat for bears. In general, though, ecotourism is considered a good way to link the well-being of people and bears, a link that may be vital for bears' survival.

Regulated hunting

As another strategy to link human well-being to the continuing presence of bears, some biologists suggest the introduction of carefully regulated hunting. Appropriate regulation would ensure that the bear population is allowed to maintain a sustainable level. In some areas the legal and regulated sport-hunting of bears has helped local economies while providing incentive for the active management of bear populations in ways compatible with the persistence of healthy numbers of bears within populations.

The polar bear is the source of a successful ecotourism program in Churchill, Manitoba, which brings millions of dollars to the town every year.

The possibilities and potential problems associated with regulated hunting are illustrated by the experiences of Romania and Bulgaria. Romania's attempt to supplement brown bear populations for hunting was successful, but the captive-bred bears released into the mountains of Bulgaria were found to be without fear of humans, hence more likely than usual to attack people. Even so, the opportunity to hunt bears obviously did provide the necessary incentive to reintroduce bears into dwindling populations, and such active management has helped the survival of bears in many other populations today. Legal and regulated hunting also

Studying Bears with Radiotelemetry

Radiotelemetry is often used to gather information about bears that will be helpful in designing conservation plans for them. Bear participants in radiotelemetry are caught in the wild, then tranquilized to allow a radio collar to be fitted around their neck, or a small radio unit attached to an ear. These transmitting devices then send out signals that tell researchers how much distance the bears cover as they move within their habitats, where they go for hibernation, and even what their body temperatures are during hibernation. The information from the radio units can either be sent to satellites and later analyzed by researchers or collected by a person with a receiver. Radiotelemetry is an excellent method for studying bears because it allows the collection of data from a distance. Thus, the bears are not disturbed and the researchers are not usually threatened.

However, as biologist Frank C. Craighead explains in *The Track of the Grizzly,* scientists can sometimes unexpectedly meet bears when radiotracking other bears. He writes about a surprise encounter he had with a female grizzly bear and her three cubs:

As I emerged out of the sagebrush, all four grizzlies, now less than 150 feet away, abruptly rose up on their hind legs and stared intently at me, definitely startled. For a few long seconds they seemed to tower above me attempting to pick up a scent, a clue to whether I was friend, foe or food. Their behavior reflected first surprise, then curiosity, but not belligerence. That wonderful inquisitive look reassured me somewhat. Then as quickly as they had risen, they dropped down on all fours, and I sensed the crucial moment had passed. While descending the sow pivoted and took off at a run, the yearlings taking their cue from her. A tremendous sense of relief swept over me as I watched the rippling fur on their hindquarters become less distinct with distance.

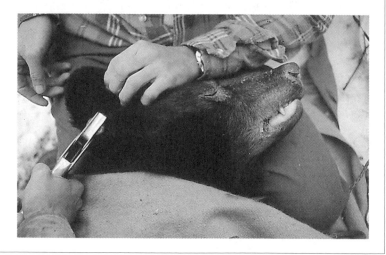

A black bear lies drugged as humans attach a small radio device to its ear. Scientists can safely study bears using radiotelemetry.

has the potential of imposed fees that can provide the funds needed to pay the personnel who enforce the regulations.

At this point, populations of some species of bear cannot tolerate any hunting at all due to their very low numbers. However, the limited hunting of polar bears, American black bears, and some populations of brown bears does appear to be feasible from a conservation standpoint, and people living in the areas where these bears are hunted appear to value the survival of bear populations.

The outlook for the bear species

Lack of knowledge about the sun bear's biology and habitat needs makes it difficult to design a conservation plan for this rare species. While it is known that sun bears cannot thrive in areas that have been converted into plantations or human settlements, they may be able to survive in areas where sustainable forestry is being practiced. If the *in situ* conservation program that the AZA recently recommended for these bears becomes a reality, it is possible that their habits will become better understood and that habitat will be secured for their preservation. However, the continuing destruction of their habitat and hunting of them for body parts make their future survival in the wild unlikely except perhaps in isolated parks and reserves.

Since the Asiatic black bear is the bear favored for use in traditional Asian medicines and foods, the future of these bears depends on whether the number killed can be controlled. Unfortunately, the information needed to effectively manage them is lacking. Although Siberia still offers large areas of undisturbed habitat, increased logging in the area now threatens this habitat. If today's trends continue, many biologists fear that the Asiatic black bears will become extinct in the near future throughout most of their range.

Although no reliable estimate of the number and distribution of sloth bears remaining in the wild exists, most of them are thought to be living on reserves in Nepal and India. This rare species is seriously threatened by encroachment

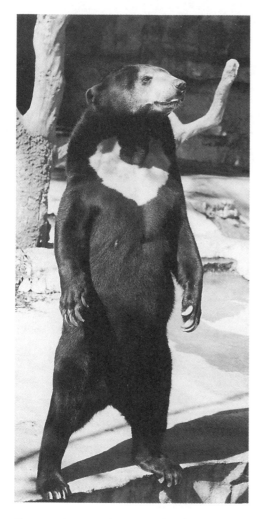

Because humans know little about sun bears in their natural habitat, the sun bear population remains especially vulnerable to extinction.

resulting from the movement of people into their habitat and by hunting for body parts.

Spectacled bears are threatened by the fragmentation of their populations as a result of human development. They are also killed for body parts and as agricultural pests. Currently, nothing is known about the distribution of the bears in many areas, and without this information effective management is impossible. Without management, and without acceptance of these bears by the local human population, spectacled bears will probably soon be extinct in the wild.

Brown bears are threatened by overhunting and habitat fragmentation, especially in Europe, most of Asia, the contiguous United States, and much of Canada. The killing of brown bears for body parts, as pests, and out of fear is responsible for their current trend of population decline. Whether promising steps taken in western Europe and Canada will be adequate to preserve bear populations is unclear. Some biologists believe that protected areas in Alaska may offer the best hope for the long-term survival of brown bears, especially because bears are a tourist attraction in these areas.

Polar bear populations are currently comparatively large since hunting has been effectively regulated. These bears have been well researched, and much is known about their distribution, population numbers, and habitat needs. However, some research shows that fewer young are surviving, and adults are thinner and smaller today than during the 1980s. Thus polar bears, too, may be facing environmental threats that endanger their future.

American black bears are still abundant in much of North America. They have been well researched and are valued by many local populations as a game species. Hunting has, overall, been successfully regulated within the limits that the bear populations can withstand. There is evidence that illegal hunting, however, may be a growing concern as poachers turn to these bears as an abundant source of body parts, especially gallbladders.

Is it possible to conserve bear species?

To conserve most, if not all, bear species would take a major commitment to research, law enforcement, and habitat protection and management. Many of the programs needed to conserve bears, like the habitat corridors being established for giant pandas in China at an estimated cost of about $10 million, are very expensive. Bears are often viewed as being in direct competition with people for natural resources, which leads to hostility toward bears in some cases, or to the view that they are a luxury we cannot afford. At this point, the survival of many populations may depend on more habitat being set aside for their use and on habitat fragments being connected by corridors. Progress toward these goals has recently been made by the governments of several countries and by the WWF and the IUCN.

For most bear populations, it is probably unrealistic to think that people will support conservation efforts aimed directly at the bears. However, it is possible that the conservation needs of bears could be met within other kinds of programs that do have the support of local populations. Examples of such programs might be sustainable forestry and the establishment of new national parks and reserves.

Sustainable forestry, in which trees are harvested in a way that allows the forest to regenerate, is especially promising as a goal consistent with bear conservation. Sustainable forestry would help preserve large tracts of forest necessary to the survival of many bear species.

The establishment of more parkland is also especially promising for bear conservation, particularly when it is adjacent to parks that already exist. In Ecuador in 1993 and 1994, the spectacled bear's habitat was improved when two new reserves were established next to the Reserve of

Cayambe-Coca. The government of Canada has recently set aside several wilderness areas that will offer protection to grizzly bears.

Quality of human life and the conservation of bears

When the "costs" of bear conservation are considered, the problem is often framed as a choice between the well-being of the humans and the well-being of bears. Christopher Servheen describes the habitat preferences shared by people and bears:

> Bears and humans have similar habitat preferences, such as valley floors where soils are fertile and access is easy. The regions where wild food for bears is available and at its most abundant are also likely to be where crops and livestock will be raised most successfully and, in turn, where people will want to establish farms and settlements.[14]

A grizzly bear stands in Glacier National Park, Montana. Glacier and Yellowstone National Parks both provide large protected areas where grizzly bear populations continue to survive.

Will protecting enough habitat to sustain bears interfere with the ability of the human population to survive and maintain a decent standard of living? Or is human well-being consistent with habitat preservation?

Many people feel that their quality of life is linked to the preservation of natural areas. Striking evidence of this is the growth and prosperity of the Greater Yellowstone ecosystem of the United States, and the twenty counties that surround it. This area consists of large amounts of land protected from development, logging, and mining, and this ecosystem is one of the few in the contiguous forty-eight states that continue to sustain grizzly bear populations.

The Greater Yellowstone area has been extremely prosperous in the past thirty years. It has experienced more growth in the number of jobs available and more growth in the average income of people living in the area than has the United States as a whole. This economic prosperity appears to have occurred because the beauty of the area attracts people and their businesses and keeps them there. However, more people near bear habitat can increase human-bear conflict, raising again the possibility that human population increases in areas close to bear habitat will actually threaten the survival of bears.

Sustainable use of natural resources and the conservation of bears

The economy of the Greater Yellowstone ecosystem is doing very well, and the vast majority of jobs are in industries such as medicine, software development, engineering, and business service. In places where the primary industries are farming, ranching, mining, or logging, the land is more likely to be used in a manner that will not preserve habitat for bears, and the protection of bear habitat is more likely to be viewed as incompatible with the economic well-being of the human population, at least in the short term.

On the other hand, there is a growing realization that forest resources are being used up. Thus in 1992, the United Nations Conference on Environment and Development

Bears as "Umbrella Species"

Some biologists think that in the temperate regions of the Northern Hemisphere, setting aside areas big enough to sustain grizzly bears would also protect most other animal and plant species occurring in the area. If this is true, then grizzlies could be considered an "umbrella species" whose protection would offer shelter to other species as well. In 1992, the Wilderness Society published a report in which a biologist mapped out a large area in Idaho that seemed to be capable of sustaining grizzly bears. A few years later, a team of scientists from Hornocker Wildlife Research Institute, the University of Idaho, and the University of Calgary discovered that the area offered a good umbrella to Idaho's mammals, birds, amphibians, and vegetation species. The only group not well covered was reptiles. Bear conservationists are interested in this kind of information because it links the conservation of bears to the conservation of other species.

(also called the Earth Summit) was held in Rio de Janeiro, Brazil. The purpose of the conference was to set out a worldwide strategy for the sustainable use of natural resources. The fact that this conference was held, and attended by many world leaders, indicates that the degradation of the environment, including the decline of biodiversity, is currently perceived as a threat to the quality of human life. Unfortunately, there has been little progress toward the goals discussed at the Earth Summit, and natural resources continue to be depleted at a rapid rate, threatening the survival of many species.

In the end, many human choices will contribute to determining whether bears, and the natural areas needed to sustain them, will continue to exist into the future. The efforts and successes in bear conservation thus far demonstrate that the survival of bears is a priority for some people. Whether their concern and efforts will ultimately result in self-sustaining bear populations depends largely on whether the people living in the same areas as bears see the bears' survival as compatible with their own well-being.

Notes

Introduction

1. Quoted in Ian Stirling, ed., *Bears: Majestic Creatures of the Wild.* Emmaus, PA: Rodale Press, 1993, p. 183.

Chapter 1: Bears of the World

2. Helen Gilks, *Bears.* New York: Ticknor and Fields, 1993, p. 11.
3. Quoted in Stirling, ed., *Bears: Majestic Creatures of the Wild,* p. 85.

Chapter 2: Habitat Destruction and Protected Lands

4. Quoted in T. H. Watkins, "National Parks, National Paradox," *Audubon,* July/August 1997, p. 42.
5. Christopher Servheen, *The Status and Conservation of the Bears of the World.* Victoria, British Columbia: International Association of Bear Research and Management, Monograph Series No. 2, 1990, p. 5.
6. Quoted in Watkins, "National Parks, National Paradox," p. 42.
7. Servheen, *The Status and Conservation of the Bears of the World,* p. 5.

Chapter 3: Hunting and the International Trade

8. Steven A. Primm, "A Pragmatic Approach to Grizzly Bear Conservation," *Conservation Biology,* vol. 10, no. 4, August 1996, p. 1026.
9. Quoted in Stirling, ed., *Bears: Majestic Creatures of the Wild,* p. 178.
10. Quoted in Stirling, ed., *Bears: Majestic Creatures of the Wild,* p. 176.

Chapter 4: Captivity and Reintroduction

11. Quoted in Stirling, ed., *Bears: Majestic Creatures of the Wild,* p. 222.

12. Quoted in Doug Peacock, "Making the West Safe for Grizzlies," *Audubon,* November/December 1997, p. 50.

Chapter 5: The Future of the Bear

13. Stephen R. Kellert, Matthew Black, Colleen Reid Rush, and Alistair J. Bath, "Human Culture and Large Carnivore Conservation in North America," *Conservation Biology,* vol. 10, no. 4, August 1996, p. 987.

14. Quoted in Stirling, ed., *Bears: Majestic Creatures of the Wild,* p. 214.

Glossary

albinism: Absence of pigmentation in an animal or plant. Animals with this condition have pale skin, light hair, and pink eyes.

AZA: American Zoo and Aquarium Association.

bear farming: Keeping and breeding bears in captivity in order to extract bile from their gallbladders for use in traditional Asian medicines.

bile: A fluid secreted by the liver to help the body absorb and digest fats.

bioaccumulation: The buildup of environmental toxins in the bodies of animals high on the food chain, from feeding on animals lower in the food chain.

biodiversity: The number of different species that exist.

bromeliad: Tropical plant belonging to a family of herbs and small plants able to survive dry spells; a major food source for spectacled bears.

captive breeding: The practice of keeping and breeding animals in captivity.

carnivore: An animal whose diet consists mainly of other animals; or a mammal belonging to the taxonomic order Carnivora, which includes bears.

catheter: A hollow tube inserted into the body to drain fluid from a body cavity or organ.

chlordane: An insecticide used to kill termites and other household and agricultural pests; no longer approved for use in the United States because it has been linked to cancer and infertility.

CITES: The Convention on International Trade in Endangered Species of Wild Fauna and Flora. An international agreement to prevent trade in endangered and threatened species if it would be detrimental to their survival.

conservation: The preservation and protection of a natural resource or wildlife species.

contiguous United States: Every state in the United States except Alaska and Hawaii.

corridors: Tracts or passageways of land that animals can use to travel back and forth between areas of high-quality habitat.

DDT: An insecticide used to kill mosquitoes and agricultural pests; banned in the United States when it was linked to cancer and reproductive problems in animals.

deforestation: The cutting down of large areas of forest, often to clear land for human settlement, farms, or pastures where livestock can graze.

dispersal: Movement from one place to another that results in the spreading out of animals within a population.

ecosystem: All of the organisms within a given area and their physical environments.

ecotourism: Tourism motivated by the desire to see ecological features such as wildlands and wildlife.

endangered: A term describing an animal or plant that is likely to become extinct in the near future.

ex situ **preservation:** Off-site preservation; preserving animal or plant species or individuals in an area other than where they usually live, especially in captivity.

extinct: A term describing an animal or plant that no longer exists because the last individual of its species has died.

food chain: A series or "chain" of species whereby each uses a "lower" species as a food source. Plants usually appear at the "bottom" of the food chain because they obtain energy from the sun instead of by eating other organisms. Large carnivores usually appear at the "top" because they feed on animals that have fed on other animals.

foraging: Searching for food.

gallbladder: An organ that stores bile from the liver.

genetic: Having to do with heredity or traits that animals and plants pass on to their offspring.

genetic variability: The amount of variation or difference that is found in the hereditary material among individuals of a species in a population.

genus: A biological category that is used to divide the members of a more general category (called a family) into different groups based on how closely related they are.

global warming: The increase in global temperatures resulting from increased levels of carbon dioxide in the atmosphere.

habitat: The native environment of an animal or plant; the kind of place where an animal or plant lives, which provides the elements it needs for survival.

habitat fragmentation: The separation of tracts of habitat that results when the areas between them become unfit for the survival of a species that usually occupies the habitat.

hibernation: A long period of inactivity in the winter when bears retreat into a den and survive by metabolizing stored fat. Females of bear species that hibernate give birth during hibernation.

home range: The area that an animal occupies or travels through during a year.

inbreeding: Reproduction that occurs among very closely related individuals; leads to low genetic variability because offspring inherit similar characteristics from both parents.

inbreeding depression: The appearance of abnormalities in individuals of an inbred population, such as physical abnormalities and reduced survival of offspring.

***in situ* preservation:** On-site preservation; preserving animal or plant species or individuals within their native environment.

IUCN: The International Union for the Conservation of Nature and Natural Resources; also called the World Conservation Union. A group composed of scientists, governments, and conservation organizations worldwide that publishes a list of threatened and endangered species and works on projects aimed at conserving natural resources.

logging: The process or business of cutting down large numbers of trees and transporting them to sawmills.

PCBs: Polychlorinated biphenyls, industrial chemicals used to make paints, adhesives, and other such products. PCBs were banned in the United States when they were linked to cancer, nerve disorders, infertility, and liver problems.

pedigree: A table, chart, or list showing ancestry or family lineage of an individual.

phytoplankton: Plants and plantlike organisms that float near the surface of the water in oceans and make up the bottom of the food chain in polar areas.

plantation: A farm, especially in a tropical area, where a crop such as coffee, cotton, or fruit is cultivated.

poaching: The illegal hunting or stealing of animals that are then sold live to unscrupulous or unknowing buyers, or killed for their body parts.

population: All the individuals of one species that occupy an area.

radiotelemetry: A method of gathering information about an animal from a distance by attaching to it a radio unit that sends signals to a receiver. These signals can be analyzed to figure out where the animal is, how active it is, and what its body temperature is.

reintroduction: Returning an animal or plant species to an area it once occupied.

self-sustaining population: A population that is large and healthy enough to continue to exist far into the future.

species: Biological categories used to divide the members of a genus into different groups, based on how closely related they are. Species is the most specific biological category and members of a species will form populations of interbreeding individuals.

Species Survival Plan: An international effort sponsored by the AZA to ensure that populations of selected species maintain enough genetic variability to continue to exist into the future. This plan includes captive breeding as well as efforts to conserve wild habitats.

stereotypy: An abnormal behavior that animals in captive situations may display, such as pacing.

studbook: A book containing pedigrees of members of a species held in captivity; these records can be used to identify suitable mates for captive-breeding programs.

sustainable forestry: Harvesting trees in such a manner that the forest will continue to exist.

sustainable use: Using resources in a way that will not exhaust them.

territory: An area occupied by an animal. This term is often used to refer to the part of the home range that an animal defends from others of its own species who might compete with it for resources.

threatened: A term used to describe a species at risk of becoming endangered if its life and/or habitat is not protected.

UDCA: Ursodeoxycholic acid, a substance that has medicinal properties and is found in comparatively high concentrations in the bile of bears. UDCA is used in Asian traditional medicines as well as in Western medicine. It can also be synthesized from cow bile.

U.S. Endangered Species Act: An act passed into law by the U.S. Congress in 1973. This act is designed to protect species at risk of extinction by preventing their hunting and protecting their habitat. The grizzly bear and the Louisiana black bear are protected by the Endangered Species Act.

viable: Capable of surviving.

vulnerable: A term used by the IUCN to describe an animal that is facing a high risk of extinction in the wild in the medium-term future.

weaned: A term used to describe a young mammal that no longer depends on its mother's milk for food.

WWF: World Wide Fund for Nature, often referred to in the United States and Canada as the World Wildlife Fund. WWF is the largest independent conservation organization and is involved in the conservation of natural resources, including bears, worldwide.

Organizations
to Contact

American Wildlands
40 East Main St., #2
Bozeman, MT 59715
(406) 586-8175
e-mail: webmail@wildlands.org
Internet: www.mcn.net/~amwild/

The mission of this organization is to protect biodiversity and encourage sustainable management of the wildlands and wildlife of the American West. Among the projects of American Wildlands is the identification and protection of movement corridors for wildlife, including bears, in the Rocky Mountains.

American Zoo and Aquarium Association (AZA)
AZA Executive Offices
7970-D Old Georgetown Rd.
Bethesda, MD 20814
(301) 907-7777
Internet: www.aza.org

The AZA, representing the zoos and aquaria in North America, sponsors the Species Survival Plan, which involves the captive breeding of endangered animals and conservation of their wild habitat. Spectacled bears, sun bears, and sloth bears are included in the Species Survival Plan.

Defenders of Wildlife
1101 14th St. NW, #1400
Washington, DC 20005
(202) 682-9400

e-mail: webmaster@defenders.org
Internet: www.defenders.org/index.html

This organization, dedicated to the protection of all native North American animals and plants, is active in work designed to ensure the survival of bears in North America. Current projects include protecting the habitat of the Florida black bear.

International Association for Bear Research and Management (IBA)

2841 Forest Ave.
Berkeley, CA 94705
fax: (510) 549-3116
e-mail: ucumari@aol.com
Internet: weber.u.washington.edu/~hammill/iba/iba.html

The IBA is an organization of biologists, wildlife managers, and others interested in the conservation of bears. This group works for the preservation of bear species through research and the distribution of information. The IBA publishes *International Bear News,* which is the newsletter of the IBA and the IUCN Bear Specialist Group.

The Predator Project

Box 6733
Bozeman, MT 59771
(406) 587-3389
e-mail: predproj@montana.avicom.net
Internet: www.wildrockies.org/predproj/

The Predator Project works to restore healthy ecosystems by protecting predators, including bears, and their habitats. This organization focuses on the area of the northern Rockies, and the northwest and northern plains regions of the United States. Projects pertaining to bears include work to close and obliterate inappropriate roads.

The World Conservation Union (IUCN), Bear Specialist Group

(The IUCN is also known as the International Union for the Conservation of Nature and Natural Resources)

U.S. Fish and Wildlife Service
University Hall, Room 309
University of Montana
Missoula, MT 59812
(406) 243-4903
e-mail: grizzly@selway.umt.edu
Internet for the IUCN: www.iucn.org

The mission of the IUCN is to influence, encourage, and assist societies all over the world in the conservation of nature. The Bear Specialist Group works to preserve bears and their habitats.

World Wide Fund For Nature (WWF)
(Known as the World Wildlife Fund in the United States and Canada)
United States Office:
1250 24th St. NW
Washington, DC 20037
(202) 293-4800
e-mail: wwfus@worldwildlife.org
Internet: www.panda.org/

The WWF combines fieldwork and policy work to conserve the natural environment worldwide. They work to conserve many bear species, including the brown bear in Europe and Russia and the giant panda in China. The WWF is the world's largest independent conservation organization.

Suggestions for Further Reading

Gary Brown, *The Great Bear Almanac.* New York: Lyons and Burford, 1993. A collection of what is known about bears, with information presented in easy-to-interpret tables and charts. Topics covered include the future of bears, names and taxonomy, bears and people, behavior, biology, and more.

Stephen Herrero, *Bear Attacks: Their Causes and Avoidance.* Edmonton, Alberta: Hurtig Publishers, 1985, 1988. An informative look at some of the reasons that people are injured and killed by grizzly and American black bears, and how these encounters might be avoided. The case study format makes for interesting reading.

George B. Schaller, *The Last Panda.* Chicago: University of Chicago Press, 1993. A document of the efforts to preserve the giant panda in the Wolong and Tangjiahe reserves of China.

Brenda Stalcup, ed., *Endangered Species: Opposing Viewpoints.* San Diego: Greenhaven Press, 1996. A collection of short articles presenting both sides of such questions as "Is extinction a serious problem?" and "Should endangered species take priority over jobs, development, and property rights?"

Ian Stirling, ed., *Bears: Majestic Creatures of the Wild.* Emmaus, PA: Rodale Press, 1993. A compilation of short articles about bears, including evolutionary history, biology, ecology, and conservation. Excellent color photographs and clear, interesting text.

Additional Works Consulted

Books

Tim W. Clark, Richard P. Reading, and Alice L. Clark, eds., *Endangered Species Recovery: Finding the Lessons, Improving the Process.* Washington, DC: Island Press, 1994. Presents case studies of efforts to conserve endangered species in the United States and analyzes why these efforts have or have not been successful. Includes a section on the Yellowstone grizzlies.

Sarah Fitzgerald, *International Wildlife Trade: Whose Business Is It?* Washington, DC: World Wildlife Fund, 1989. A presentation of the harmful impacts of international trade in wildlife and the efforts to control this trade through the Convention on International Trade in Endangered Species of Wild Fauna and Flora (CITES). Includes sections on land mammals, aquatic mammals, birds, reptiles, and plants.

Helen Gilks, *Bears.* New York: Ticknor and Fields, 1993. An illustrated book for younger readers about the physical characteristics and behavior of the bears of the world. Information about human-bear interactions and conservation is also included.

David Macdonald, ed., *The Encyclopedia of Mammals.* New York: Facts On File Publications, 1987. An encyclopedia that includes information about all known mammal species. Entries are written for general audiences by scientists involved in mammal research. Conservation and new or developing theories are highlighted.

Catherine McCracken, Debra A. Rose, and Kurt A. Johnson, *Status, Management, and Commercialization of the American Black Bear (Ursus americanus)*. Traffic USA, published in cooperation with the World Wildlife Fund, 1995. Details the current status of the American black bear with an emphasis on laws protecting them, population estimates, and threats to their survival arising from the international trade in bear parts.

Gary K. Meffe, C. Ronald Carroll, and contributors, *Principles of Conservation Biology*. Sunderland, MA: Sinauer Associates, Inc., 1994. Written for a scientific audience, this book presents principles of conservation biology such as the management of populations for genetic variation. It also includes essays by scientists presenting their research on issues pertaining to species conservation.

Christopher Servheen, *The Status and Conservation of the Bears of the World*. Victoria, British Columbia: International Association of Bear Research and Management, Monograph Series No. 2, 1990. A report on the distribution and population estimates of each bear species. Information on the threats faced by each species, the laws protecting them, and effectiveness of these laws is also included, with each country that bears inhabit discussed separately. Written for a scientific audience.

Periodicals and newsletters

"Bear Translocation Plan," *Oryx,* vol. 28, no. 3, 1994.

Bonnie M. Blanchard and Richard R. Knight, "Biological Consequences of Relocating Grizzly Bears in the Yellowstone Ecosystem," *Journal of Wildlife Management,* vol. 59, no. 3, 1995.

Adele Conover, "He's Just One of the Bears," *National Wildlife,* vol. 30, June/July 1992.

Kare Elgmork, "The Brown Bear *Ursus arctos L.* in Norway: Assessment of Status Around 1990," *Biological Conservation,* vol. 78, 1996.

John L. Eliot, "Polar Bears: Stalkers of the High Arctic," *National Geographic,* vol. 193, no. 1, January 1998.

Goran Ewald, Per Larsson, Henric Linge, Lennart Okla, and Nicole Szarzi, "Biotransport of Organic Pollutants to an Inland Alaska Lake by Migrating Sockeye Salmon *(Oncorhynchus nerka),*" *Arctic,* vol. 51, no. 1, March 1998.

"Field Notes," *The Bear Specialist Group Newsletter,* vol. 1, no. 3, 1993.

"France Seeks Bears," *Oryx,* vol. 28, no. 4, 1994.

Warren Getler, "The Polar Bear Slides," *Audubon,* May/June 1997.

Anup R. Joshi, David L. Garshelis, and James L. D. Smith, "Home Ranges of Sloth Bears in Nepal: Implications for Conservation," *Journal of Wildlife Management,* vol. 59, no. 2, 1995.

Stephen R. Kellert, Matthew Black, Colleen Reid Rush, and Alistair J. Bath, "Human Culture and Large Carnivore Conservation in North America," *Conservation Biology,* vol. 10, no. 4, August 1996.

F. Knauer, et al., "A Recovery Plan for Brown Bears in the Trenton Alps, Council of Europe," *Environmental Encounters,* vol. 17, 1994.

Linda Laikre, Robert Andren, Hans-Ove Larsson, and Nils Ryman, "Inbreeding Depression in Brown Bear *Ursus arctos,*" *Biological Conservation,* vol. 76, 1996.

Sid Marty, "Homeless on the Range: Grizzlies Struggle for Elbow Room and Survival in Banff National Park," *Canadian Geographic,* January/February 1997.

Downs Matthews and Ian Higginson, "Dan Guravich (1918–1997)," *Arctic,* vol. 51, no. 2, June 1998.

Francois Messier, Mitchell K. Taylor, and Malcolm A. Ramsay, "Denning Ecology of Polar Bears in the Canadian Arctic Archipelago," *Journal of Mammology,* vol. 75, no. 2, May 1994.

Reed F. Noss, Howard B. Quigley, Maurice G. Hornocker, Troy Merrill, and Paul C. Paquet, "Conservation Biology and Carnivore Conservation in the Rocky Mountains," *Conservation Biology,* vol. 10, no. 4, August 1996.

Madan K. Oli, Harry A. Jacobson, and Bruce D. Leopold, "Denning Ecology of Black Bears in the White River National Wildlife Refuge, Arkansas," *Journal of Wildlife Management,* vol. 61, no. 3, 1997.

Doug Peacock, "Making the West Safe for Grizzlies," *Audubon,* November/December 1997.

B. Peyton, "The Status of the Spectacled Bear," *International Bear News,* vol. 4, no. 1, 1995.

Steven A. Primm, "A Pragmatic Approach to Grizzly Bear Conservation," *Conservation Biology,* vol. 10, no. 4, August 1996.

David Quammen, "Island of the Bears," *Audubon,* March/April 1995.

Raymond Rasker and Arlin Hackman, "Economic Development and the Conservation of Large Carnivores," *Conservation Biology,* vol. 10, no. 4, August 1996.

Christopher Servheen, *IUCN/Species Survival Commission (SSC) Bear Specialist Group Newsletter,* no. 1, January 1990.

———, *IUCN/SSC Bear Specialist Group Newsletter,* no. 2, February 1991.

Mary-Powel Thomas, "Climate Change Hits Home," *Audubon,* September/October 1997.

Kimberly Titus and LaVerne Beier, "The Brown Bears of Admiralty Island," *Alaska Geographic,* vol. 18, no. 3, 1991.

T. H. Watkins, "National Parks, National Paradox," *Audubon,* July/August 1997.

William Weber and Alan Rabinowitz, "A Global Perspective on Large Carnivore Conservation," *Conservation Biology,* vol. 10, no. 4, August 1996.

Robert B. Wielgus and Fred L. Bunnell, "Tests of Hypotheses for Sexual Segregation in Grizzly Bears," *Journal of Wildlife Management,* vol. 59, no. 3, 1995.

Reports, news releases, and factsheets

American Zoo and Aquarium Association, Bear Advisory Group, "Bear Species," 1997.

Kathy Carlstead, John Seidensticker, and Robert Baldwin, "Environmental Enrichment for Zoo Bears," unpublished manuscript, National Zoological Park, Smithsonian Institution, Washington, DC, date unknown.

Interagency Grizzly Bear Committee, "Grizzly Bear Compendium," Washington, DC: The National Wildlife Federation, 1987.

IUCN, "Red List of Threatened and Endangered Animals," 1996.

IUDZN/CBSG (IUCN/SSC), "The World Zoo Conservation Strategy: The Role of the Zoos and Aquaria of the World in Global Conservation," 1993.

National Wildlife Federation, "News Release: Poll Shows Support for Citizen Management of Grizzly Bears in the Bitterroot," June 11, 1997.

U.S. Fish and Wildlife Service, "Draft Environmental Impact Statement: Grizzly Bear Recovery in the Bitterroot Ecosystem," 1997.

———, "Louisiana Black Bear Recovery Plan," Jackson, Mississippi, 1995.

World Wildlife Fund Canada, "The Black Bear and Illegal Trade in Bear Parts," factsheets, 1996.

"WWF International Country Profile: China," 1995.

Index

Picture Credits

About the Author

Laura Barghusen is a Midwestern author with a strong interest in endangered species and other ecological issues. With a background in zoology, she is a writer of science educational materials as well as an artist who has illustrated books about animals. While working as a seasonal ranger with the U.S. National Park Service, she had the opportunity to see black bears in the wild and to compile information about the locations where bears were sighted in a Northwestern park.